Business Ground Rules for HVAC Contractors

100 Lessons for Success

Clovercroft/Publishing

Business Ground Rules for HVAC Contractors: 100 Lessons for Success

© 2014 by Mitsubishi Electric US

Published by Clovercroft Publishing, Franklin, Tennessee

Cover Design by Debbie Manning Sheppard

Interior Layout Design by Suzanne Lawing

Printed in the United States of America

9781940262581

Foreword

This book isn't a manual.
It is 100 best practices every contractor needs to know.

Tony Jeary is a world-renowned expert who helps people get results, and he has worked with us for many years. When he came to us with this great idea, I knew it would be a winning opportunity. Because of the positive response he and his co-author Peter Thomas have had with their book, *Business Ground Rules*, he suggested that he do a book specifically for HVAC contractors—that's what you have in your hands. The message and principles discussed in this book align with many of Mitsubishi Electric, U.S. Cooling & Heating's priorities in relation to our contractors, and we agreed to sponsor the book and make it available for our contractor community.

This is a very exciting and dynamic time in the HVAC industry. Together with our contractors, we are pioneering customized comfort. Our technology is revolutionizing how comfort is achieved through individual room control and energy savings.

There are many challenges in the industry today, including a high attrition rate. Often owners begin as technicians and decide to start their own business. While they may be initially successful, many struggle with managing a business or marketing themselves effectively, causing sales to suffer. My goal is that the 100 best practices found in this book will help contractors either expand their businesses or become more profitable, or both.

These best practices come from many subject-matter experts inside and outside of our industry. Some are gleaned from Tony and Peter's exceptional experiences with entrepreneurs and out-of-the-box thinkers. Others are solid examples of innovation, creativity, and persistence from some of the greatest minds I've crossed paths with in my career—successful business people across different industries. While you may not feel the need to apply all 100 practices to your own business, I know you'll find some great ideas to help motivate, organize, and streamline your operations while increasing your bottom line.

Inside, you'll find unique concepts and suggestions, real-life examples, pictures and templates, and references to additional training—all in bite-sized portions. As you use this book as a daily reference guide of best practices, be strategic. Apply these best practices toward three foundational pillars of success: clarity, focus, and execution. Above all, remember that it's all about our customers. This business was built on relationships, and it will thrive or die based on relationships we cultivate and our ability to add value.

There's a lot of competition out there, but revolutionary technologies, such as ductless and variable refrigerant flow, are creating tremendous opportunities for contractors. Since contractors are the core of our company, we at Mitsubishi Electric, U.S. Cooling & Heating, are committed to helping our contractors win. Whether you're hiring new people, utilizing our equipment, or wanting to streamline your daily processes, I hope this book makes it easier for you to do business and get better results.

Allan Dziwoki
Senior Vice President – Sales, Marketing, and Operations
Mitsubishi Electric, U.S. Cooling & Heating

Contents

STRATEGIC

FOCUS

BRAND, MARKETING & SALES

LEADERSHIP

PEOPLE

Introduction

This is a special book. It's not designed to be read cover to cover in one sitting. It's really designed to be a tool to help you, as a business owner (a contractor), to be more successful.

These 100 rules, lessons, and great ideas will help you sharpen your business efforts so you can prosper faster, yield more from your efforts, and build upon whatever size business you currently have. We are committed to keeping each item short, using pictures and charts where applicable, for a fast but informative read. We've even teamed up with Mitsubishi Electric, Cooling & Heating, so you can have even more tools with a free downloadable tool chest that complements this book.

We hope you either start teaming up with Mitsubishi Electric, U.S. Cooling & Heating, or that you expand your relationship with the company. ME ductless is like no other product, and the company is full of special people committed to all stakeholders winning—and that includes you, the contractor who touches the customer.

In today's fast-paced world every business owner and leader is looking for things they can do better, ways they can think and process more efficiently, and systems they can put in place to yield immediate wins. We hope this book is a multiplier for you, so read on. Study those items that grab your attention and learn how to become even more successful.

THINKING

1.
Live Life on Purpose

*Living life intentionally and fully will help keep you
on the right path to success.*

Sure, good things can happen by accident. We've all found something delightful and forgotten in a coat pocket or under the sofa cushion. Finding extra money is good. Finding a lost key is good. But in our daily lives, is "good" really good enough?

High achievers don't settle for good; they seek awesome. And truly awesome things—hard-won and positive accomplishments—happen on purpose, as a result of thoughtful self-reflection, strong planning, and focused effort.

> HIGH ACHIEVERS DON'T SETTLE FOR GOOD; THEY SEEK *AWESOME.*

Measurement matters, and reflecting on the personal accomplishments in your life every once in a while (both past and present) can be motivating and inspiring. Measurement is an important step of living your life on purpose and developing your future. Both Peter and Tony have pages and pages of literally hundreds of goals they have both set and met throughout their lifetimes. There is real power in documenting dreams and keeping an inventory of successes; life rarely happens the way you want it to by chance.

To start living your life on purpose, simply craft a list of valuable milestones you've already achieved. Whether you ran a marathon, earned a degree, met and married the partner of your dreams, established a company, or mastered juggling, begin making your list of the things you've already accomplished. Document realized educational goals, financial successes, personal accomplishments, and any other moments when your hard work has paid off.

Over time, it may become more formalized and find itself in chronological order as you meet new goals; but for now, simply take some time to look back on your undertakings, deeds, and successes. Going forward, you can organize it chronologically, by subject, or by importance. What's essential here is taking stock of how you've already lived a life of purpose, even if you weren't aware of it with this mindset. Reading through proof of your past achievements can be an important nudge when you need encouragement.

Likewise, browsing through documentation of where you've been and what you've done can be a powerful springboard for more purposeful success.

Now consider a few more questions: What do you want more of? Where would you rather be? Is there something of note you want to earn? How's the health of your bucket list?

> COMMIT TO "MARGIN TIME" IN YOUR CALENDAR FOR THINKING, FLEXIBILITY, AND HEALTH-RELATED ACTIVITIES.
> –TONY JEARY

Asking yourself these kinds of introspective questions—and writing down the answers—will allow you to make smart changes and strategic decisions that will purposely propel you forward toward what you most want to accomplish, whatever the scope or size.

Don't become sidetracked with trying to create a perfect and complete list before starting; the best way to get to work is simply to get to work! Focus on a goal you've documented. You can choose the easiest one, or maybe the most enticing—whatever best suits your motivation. Write down what needs to happen in order for that goal to be a success. Identify anyone who can, will, or should help you. And be sure to give yourself a deadline so that you create a little positive anxiety about reaching your goal. Now, get going. It really is as simple as that.

Solid accomplishments are so much better than happy accidents, and that's a distinction that truly successful people know and live—on purpose.

2.
Acknowledge Your Core Beliefs

We all have core beliefs that shape the way we operate our life. Understanding them will help guide you to have good balance between your beliefs and how you lead your life.

What is your belief system? This is a complex question that only you can answer, even though the answer itself might be incredibly simple. What are the core beliefs that drive the way you live and operate your life?

Core beliefs are at the core of who you are as a person, the way you filter the world. You have principles that you've acquired and formed through the years. Being aware of these principles strongly affects your results.

Think about all the different ways your beliefs are formed over time. As a child, your beliefs are learned from your parents and will be shaped by other influences, including school, work, TV, media, reading, mentors, ethnic culture, church, and politics.

> "BE CLEAR ON THE BELIEFS THAT YOU FILTER YOUR LIFE BY."
> –TONY JEARY

As you grow into adulthood, you often end up challenging your belief on something that you took at face value when you were younger, because now you have more information; and that's a good thing.

What are some of the main beliefs that shape the way you operate your life?

Beliefs really do have an impact on your results; so the sooner you acknowledge those beliefs, the sooner you can begin to align your life and business accordingly.

3.
Eliminate Blind Spots from Your Belief Window

Be open minded to changing how you've always done something or thought about it to eliminate Blind Spots and roadblocks that keep you from moving forward (i.e., the value of ductless).

Your Belief Window is how you perceive and understand everything in your life—the way you see the world, your role in that world, and the relationships you have with others. It includes everything you believe to be true, false, correct, incorrect, appropriate, inappropriate, possible, and impossible. It frames all your views of people, places, and things, and creates the perceptions and feelings you have about everything. It also influences the actions you take regarding those same people, places, and things. This window allows information you consider important to enter your mind and be retained, and blocks out the things that you do not consider important. It screens information and circumstances you don't think you need.

> OUR *BELIEF WINDOW* CONTAINS THE PRINCIPLES WE BELIEVE TO BE TRUE. CONSTANTLY CHECK FOR BLIND SPOTS, DISTINCTIONS, AND PERSPECTIVES TO ENSURE YOUR PRINCIPLES ARE ACCURATE AND UP TO DATE.
>
> –TONY JEARY

We all have Blind Spots that obscure what we could and should see past, and these can really hinder results. Sometimes principles that cross our Belief Window can be wrong, outdated, or limiting. How are we to know what our Blind Spots are so we can expand our frame of reference? I believe there are four core ways to do this:

1) Engage a mentor to pour into you.
2) Hire a coach to sharpen your thinking.
3) Reach out to trusted colleagues.
4) Feed your mind purposefully through books, videos, and audios.

High achievers realize that they need and want to know more about topics relevant to their success, and they keep themselves relevant and updated through conscious effort. This conscious learning and investigation will help expand your Belief Window, which, in turn, will help you make smarter decisions.

Take a good look at your Belief Window and do some refinement. Get the opinion or perspective of a trusted coach, and intentionally expand your knowledge base on things important to you. Once you clean off those old, incorrect principles and misconceptions from your window, you'll see so much farther and your success will exponentially increase.

Keep an open mind and constantly look for help to see opportunities. Change can be good if implemented in the correct way. For example, many AC contractors have had a blind spot on how valuable ductless can be to their offerings, to their yield, and their profitability.

WRONG BELIEFS
INHIBIT RESULTS

4.
Select Mentors Carefully and Have Them Help You Think Smart

"Seek out mentors who've accomplished what you want to accomplish, whether they are other contractors or not. Have several mentors for balance."

Is there something in your business you want to improve? Is there a new sector your want to get into? Do you want to grow your business? A mentor can help you with all of these areas and more.

- Mentors support and encourage you to maximize your potential.
- Mentoring helps you look at yourself and opportunities so you can decide what you want or which direction to take.
- Issues between mentor and mentee are confidential.
- Mentoring helps turn decisions into action.

Yes, you need a mentor—preferably more than one. If you do not have any, it's time to get some. Compile a list of prospective mentors—ask your banker, your accountant, your lawyer, and folks around town who are wired into the small-business community for the names of veteran small-business owners who may be interested in helping you succeed; they don't have to be AC contractors.

You can only be as successful as your own mind allows you to be, if you act alone. Entrepreneurs are often used to going it alone; but if you want to be more successful than you currently are, you'll have to rely on others to get you there. Mentors can be a phenomenal resource because the right ones have traveled the journey that you are embarking on. There's always someone with more wisdom and knowledge than you to learn from.

Remember that the most successful entrepreneurs are willing to learn. They never assume they know it all or have all the answers. If you want to grow and advance faster, be intentional about your mentors and coaches. Don't just work with mentors you know and like; find someone who's doing what you want to do, even if you don't know the person.

Who are your mentors in business or in life in general? A mentor isn't necessarily a family member or a friend. This person is not necessarily a coach, either, because a mentor offers his or her wisdom for free. This person is someone who is willing to give you advice about how to run your business, attract more clients, or implement certain valuable processes. Every mentoring session should include a discussion that uncovers options, solutions, and new ideas.

> ## THERE'S ALWAYS SOMEONE WITH MORE WISDOM AND KNOWLEDGE THAN YOU TO LEARN FROM.

Mentors give back. They want to give back to the world and they want to give advice, because it is part of their legacy and contribution. We recommend having at least five mentors, since both of us have personally benefited immensely from mentor-mentee relationships. Even though Tony is a world-renowned business strategist, has owned dozens of businesses, and has advised over 1,000 clients; and even though Peter is seventy-five, wealthy, and has done hundreds of deals—we both know that we don't know everything! That's what mentors are for.

I (Tony) wanted to raise exceptional kids, so I found mentors who had already achieved that. I even found mentors who had two girls, just like I do. I carefully chose those mentors who had successful daughters and asked them to share their knowledge and time with my family and me. It really is valuable to get the opinion and insight of another person who is equally committed to your success.

When I (Peter) started my first company, my lawyer told me that I needed to appoint some directors who could give the company wisdom, direction, and strategy. I was only twenty-eight years old and had not met enough people then who I felt could give me the advice that I needed, so I got creative. At home, we had a book of black-and-white photographs of John F. Kennedy, Martin Luther King, Gandhi, and Ernest Hemingway, among other famous people. I knew they had a lot of wisdom and could advise me with what I needed to do, so I cut their pictures out and framed them. As challenges came into my life, I would ask each one of them what they would do about the particular issue. I found that JFK was the business advisor. MLK was the person who could tell me what was right and what was wrong; he was a wonderful decision maker. Gandhi was my spiritual guide, and Mr. Hemingway was the writer and rogue advisor. If I wanted an excuse to have a little fun, I would be sure to ask Ernest.

The purpose of this kind of "virtual mentorship" is to open your mind to the idea that you do not need living mentors (although they are great and you should have them), but you can have access to the wisdom of the ages if you use your imagination. Once you select who your virtual mentors are going to be, immediately go down to your favorite bookstore, buy an autobiography of your first mentor, and read it cover to cover. No matter who your virtual mentor is, you can read or download something on him or her and learn.

Leverage your mentors and get as much wisdom as you can from them. By listening to and observing the habits of those more successful than yourself in selected areas and then modeling that behavior, you will constantly elevate your levels of thought and success.

And of course, be selective who you choose as mentors. Look at what they've accomplished, not just what they say. This will allow you to broaden your network of personal influencers, friends, and colleagues.

5.
Get a Coach

*Look to other experts and advisors to expand your thinking
and actions to bring positive impact to your success.*

Coaching isn't just for professional athletes. The concept of coaching has been in place for decades. Top CEOs have coaches who guide them with personal and professional advice. Entrepreneurs have coaches who challenge and inspire them to be their best. Do you have a powerful coach?

It's worth noting that a coach is different than a mentor: Coaches are paid; mentors are not. Coaches offer paid advice, while a mentor is generally free advice from someone who wants to give back. A colleague can be a trusted advisor who coaches you, but don't confuse them with a coach. Some people say, "I have a trusted colleague, so I don't need a coach." If this is your thinking, you may want to reframe it. Coaching is an investment in yourself, your business, and your results.

> **COACHING IS AN INVESTMENT IN YOURSELF, YOUR BUSINESS, AND YOUR RESULTS.**

Everyone should have one (or more) mentor. And everyone should have a coach. I (Tony) was sitting in my *Strategic Acceleration Studio* a few years back strategizing with the CIO of Deloitte; and I was saying that as of that time, I'd had the same coach for more than twenty-five years. This man was shocked. He said, "You've had the same man for twenty-five years helping you succeed in business and helping you win in life? That's longer than you've been married." I said yes. He said, "Do you know how fortunate you are to have someone in your life that long who supports you in being successful?" I had not thought about it in those terms before and appreciated his pointing this out. I needed to show more gratitude for my long-term friend and coach, Mark Pantak. This man serves up the best books, introduces me to special people, makes me aware of Blind Spots, councils me on my thinking, and sharpens my vision. He prays for my wisdom and success often. I sent him an iPad the very next day with a special note of thanks.

Successful people reach higher levels through coaches who impact their thinking. Coaches can help you reach your peak performance and operate often at higher levels—like the mastery level. A coach will expand your thinking, help you be more accountable, help minimize mistakes, and bring positive value to your success.

Choose someone who matches your values. Find an expert who already has success in your field and has proven success in the direction you want to go. Find someone who has done what you want to do, who studies, has an arsenal, has real experience, and of course has a sincere desire to help you win. You can even use your network to identify a coach.

6.
Benchmark: Research and Model Others

*Use others' successes to your advantage by understanding what they've
done that worked well and as what did not work well.
Not everything has to be an original idea.*

Benchmarking is simply looking for what's working for others and duplicating what they've done, if you're not already doing it. Effective leaders want to grow and expand as professionals while, also taking their team and organization to higher levels of results.

Benchmarking can be done by leveraging mentors, exploring industry best practices, and modeling; it should be part of a system that constantly serves up best trends, practices, technology, etc., to enable top leadership to make better decisions. Benchmarking can also come from reading and studying reports, research, and impactful books authored by authorities.

Identify those who are successful in the same line of work as you and leverage industry groups like Nextar and SGI. What are the distinctions that have helped them rise to their level of success? Here are some helpful questions to ask:

- What were their reasons for choosing their location?
- How do they get the word out about the products and services they offer?
- Who is their target market? Who do they attract?
- What are their numbers – revenues, expenses, profitability?
- How has their growth strategy played out?
- What initiatives and strategies are they pursuing now and in the future?

- What separates them from their competition?

Top leaders know their competition as well as they know their own business. Creating a data-rich competitive comparison document provides quick insight into market position and trends, strengths and weaknesses, and opportunities for change or advantage. This document should be updated regularly and can be shared with the organization, creating more mental synergy and team focus.

Benchmarking will grow your effectiveness, period!

We identified 10 items below that we believe are important to maximize your leadership and/or execution opportunities. Rate yourself on each and see where you may have areas of opportunities that can create the biggest impact for you.

Executing as a Strong Leader – Top 10

Strategic Clarity	Rating 1-10*
1. Do you create a Vision for your team or people you bring into the business so they know your priorities?	
2. Are you really creating a great Leadership Brand and reputation so that people want to follow you, based on modeling what you teach?	
3. Do you create your own Performance Standards of effectiveness; a true leader knows what makes them good and is able to share with those underneath them?	
Presentation/Communication	
4. Do you have tools all around you that make you Presentation Ready at all times? Do you clearly understand your Presentation Universe and all the opportunities in your world?	
5. Do you have established Meeting Protocol for granting appointments, calls, and meetings (avoid wasted meetings, all meetings have stated objectives and are granted, driven and focused accordingly)?	
Leadership/Communication	
6. Are you clear on what your strengths are and what you should be spending the most time doing – working in HLAs (High-Leverage Activities)?	
7. Are you constantly looking for Best Practices that are working for you and others and then duplicating things that are working, and sharing them with your team (things you're leading towards using likeness (i.e., we want our organization to like a model home, we want our office to provide service like the Ritz Carlton, etc.)?	
8. Networking/Connections – Are you networking to get to the right kind of people that are a fit? Are you putting yourself in the right places to be around people who are interested?	
Time & Energy Management	
9. Do you have good Energy Management (diet, timing, stress) - it's not just about 168 hours in a week, it's about being at peak for the top opportunities. Health and energy matter.	
10. Are you feeding your Mind/Innovation (read, listen, be coached so that you consistently model growing and improving, avoid stagnation with fresh inputs) for that you can operate at your very best?	

Rate yourself on a scale of 1-10, with 10 being the best.   **TOTAL:** _____

Actions

_____

_____

_____

_____

_____

_____

7.
Gather Information Regularly and Make Great Decisions

Accelerated results happen when you have quick access to information that allows you to make educated decisions as quickly as possible.

Getting the information you need quickly and reliably helps make great decisions. Leaders and business owners often miss the fact that they can have their staff do the research and data-gathering portion of an issue on which they need to make a decision; there's no need to rely solely on themselves to solve every issue. Using appropriate staff members to do the up front work will maximize time at the highest level and eliminate the potential for procrastination in making decisions due to time constraints.

The successful leader needs to identify and measure Critical Success Factors (CSFs) or Key Performance Indicators (KPIs) tied to the strategic plan. From there, identifying the right people to funnel the appropriate information back to them for ease in putting all the pieces together creates a platform from which to operate and execute efficiently.

Utilizing a customized dashboard that shows the real daily, weekly, and monthly results is a must. Visibility of true effectiveness will permit more nimble and targeted decision-making.

Being truthfully informed with timely and accurate information versus just viewing standard accounting reports can make the difference in winning and losing.

CLARITY

8.
Clarity: Get It And Use It

"Know what you want, then communicate this focus to your teams (i.e., in meetings, wall charts, posters in shop, vehicle signs)."

What do you want out of life? Your business? Your deals? Clarity, focus, and successful execution are essential pillars of entrepreneurism, and necessary tools for getting what you want. The most successful people design their own lives, and then live their lives on purpose. But the first step is clarity.

The definition of clarity is understanding and documenting your targets clearly and determining the "why" behind reaching them (personally and professionally). It's about developing a clear vision, outlining priorities and objectives,

> THE STRENGTH OF AN INDIVIDUAL OR TEAM OFTEN LIES IN ITS ATTITUDE, MOTIVATION, AND COMMITMENT.
> - PETER THOMAS

and tackling goals with a real sense of urgency and focus. Clarity is achieved when ideas and concepts are clearly explained and presented internally and externally; it's when we know where we are in relation to where we want to go.

When clarity is lost, or never achieved in the first place, it is almost impossible to generate the kind of focus necessary to establish a dynamic organization capable of acting swiftly and deftly on a daily basis. What you're left with instead is a struggling, underperforming organization and frustrated employees eager to jump ship.

The requirements for clarity are specific with respect to three issues:

1. **Purpose**—relates to the "why" of things, thought through and documented
2. **Value**—relates to the real benefits that can be acquired (for all stakeholders to win)
3. **Objectives**—relates to the premise that unless objectives are stated clearly and understood by all, the likelihood of achieving them is slim

You have to ask yourself the hard questions: "Why do I want to buy a franchise?" "Why do I want to be in the business I'm in?" Are you building a business to sell, or are you building a family business you want to pass down? Be clear on what you want and utilize tools along the way. (Visit www.strategicacceleration.com for a free assessment and many free tools.)

When you have an authentic vision, things happen. If you have no vision, there is nothing to tie your objectives to and nothing to measure your progress or performance against. When you have clarity about your vision, you discover yourself being pulled toward it; and all you have to do is follow the connecting opportunities that carry you along, allowing you to make connections faster.

Think about a time when you've been excited and regenerated at the thought of achieving a big goal. For an entrepreneur, there's nothing like the adrenaline rush of having complete clarity about what it is you want to achieve. When you have clarity, you get that excitement that builds and fuels your energy toward that dream. The results you achieve will often come faster than you may have thought possible.

Clarity and focus together form the basis of execution. So get completely clear about the things that you want and then take action.

Know what you want and how you want to operate; share that with your team. Then stay focused on what you want to achieve and have your employees focus the same way concerning company goals and objectives.

9.
Discover Your Strengths and Talents in Life and Business

Each human being can lay claim to something he or she has that no other person has. The exact experiences you have lived are as unique as your fingerprints or your DNA. The key is using your gifts to create wins for your life and your business.

I believe that at some point in life, most people have a dream, but something happens to it over time. Every elementary schoolchild is asked, "What do you want to be when you grow up?" If you have ever seen children confronted with this question, you see how quickly they respond, with little hesitation.

Some say, "I want to be a fireman." Some say, "I want to be a pilot." Others may say they want to be a doctor or possibly even the president of the United States. Yet very few of these schoolchildren actually live out their childhood dreams.

Did you have a childhood dream you eventually achieved? Most of us don't. As adults, many people still find themselves asking the question, "What do I want to be when I grow up?" This leads us to an obvious question we need to answer about ourselves. Was there a time in your life that you had a vision and there was something you really wanted to achieve? My guess is that you would respond yes. So what happened to you along the way, if you were unable to execute your vision?

There are two main reasons you might decide to give up on your dreams:

- The first reason is that you aren't clear about what you really want.
- The second reason is that you did not approach your opportunities properly.

You may have believed you had to do things that were big, huge, and significant. What you actually need to do is connect a series of small steps and opportunities that will eventually produce the final result you want. Go as far as you can see, and then you will see farther!

Each of us has the ability to do a particular thing and to do it very well. For some people, it may be the ability to teach and explain things. For others it might be the ability to wade into complicated situations and discern simple solutions. For others it may be the ability to write. Still others may have the gift and ability to create poetry, music, or another art form. For some it might be mechanical skill or athletic ability.

Whatever your gifts or talents may be, they can be seen as an unbroken thread throughout your life. Our talents and gifts become evident when we are young, and they continue to be refined and revealed until we die.

The most significant fact about your gifts and your talents is that they involve things you probably love to do. Think about it: Nobody has to push you to do those things. You do them because they give you pleasure and because, in doing them, you feel you have provided value for others as well as yourself.

For that reason, I believe authentic creation of a vision begins with embracing your gifts and talents that allow you to exceed others' expectations, and this works in both personal relationships and businesses.

There are certain things your business does very well, and the ability to do those things differentiates you from your competition. Understanding those advantages is critical to sustaining organizational success and effectiveness over the long haul.

Organizations have unique skills and abilities because the people who populate the organization have unique skills and abilities. In the same way that personal gifts and skills are seen throughout an individual life, they are also seen in the life of an organization.

You are defined not only by who you are, but what you excel at doing and how those talents affect others in your life. Maybe you're a skilled networker, or have an affinity for meeting deadlines. Do you really know your talents and strengths, especially as others see them? Ask people in your life what they see as your top three biggest talents (email is an easy way to do this); you might just be surprised.

Many people mistake skill for talent. Some of the most successful and skilled individuals were not necessarily "talented," but were committed to learning and acquiring a distinction or knowledge that propelled them to effective performance. What skills do you have now? What skills do you want to acquire?

When you recognize and claim your talents within the context of value creation, you will begin to see connections that lead to an authentic vision, with the power to transform your professional and personal life, and possibly the lives of many others.

10.
Have a Simple Plan

*"You need to have a plan with objectives and actions,
even if it is only one page."*

Success is very seldom about pure luck. We are successful when we achieve objectives on purpose. In other words, we have thought through our vision, are clear on what we want to achieve, and then systematically go about taking the actions that will get us where we want to go, even if it means we have to change direction. In a nutshell, this is what planning is about. If you don't create a plan, it's almost impossible to achieve your vision.

> GO AS FAR AS YOU CAN
> SEE, THEN YOU CAN
> SEE—FARTHER
> –TONY JEARY

Your plan should be a values-based strategy for the long haul. By values-based, we mean that it's critical to establish clarity about what matters most to you first as the leader, and then create your vision, mission, and objectives from your values.

Remember the great explorers Christopher Columbus and Lewis and Clark? They had a vision. They had a plan. A plan will help you navigate treacherous waters, or avoid them altogether, and help keep you focused.

Clear vision is critical to success and effectiveness, so it is easy to understand why vision is critical when you understand what success really is. We are successful when we achieve objectives we have established in advance. And how will we establish them? With a plan.

The gray shaded areas should contain your main action items, and the white areas beneath should contain the sub-actions."

#	WHAT	WHEN	WHO
	**Strategic Action Plan**		
	Overall Goal/Vision Statement:		
1.			
a.			
b.			
c.			
2.			
a.			
b.			
c.			
3.			
a.			
b.			
c.			
4.			
a.			
b.			
c.			
5.			
a.			
b.			
c.			
6.			
a.			
b.			
c.			
7.			
a.			
b.			
c.			
8.			
a.			
b.			
c.			

11.
Write Your Own Mission Statement

*A mission statement helps ensure you are clear on
why you are doing what you're doing.*

Having a mission statement (the why) and a set of goals or objectives (the targets) are important (both personal and business) in order to achieve the right results faster. We learned that every entrepreneur needs a clean and current action plan. If you don't have one, you're simply costing yourself time and money, living your business life on autopilot. That's not a way to operate.

Having a clear, concise mission statement creates wins on multiple levels. Not only does it create clarity of purpose for yourself and your entire team, but it also serves as an external statement of the key brand you are presenting to the world.

Why does your organization exist? "Why" gives you power. It forces refinement and supports prioritization. People want to know the "why."

> KEY ELEMENTS OF A MISSION STATEMENT: WHAT DO WE DO, HOW DO WE DO IT, WHOM DO WE DO IT FOR, AND WHAT VALUE WE ARE BRINGING.

Your mission statement is simply an explanation of who you are and what you're about. It should be congruent with your vision and values and should make a statement about your business strategy.

Sometimes a mission statement can be as complex as a paragraph with bullet points, and sometimes it can be as simple as a short phrase or tagline. We are big believers in simplicity and action, so we recommend keeping it on the shorter side. As briefly—yet as comprehensively—as possible, describe why your company exists and its big-picture objective(s).

Personally, my company is all about results. Therefore, my mission statement is: *Drive extraordinary results for clients and in return provide exceptional compensation that supports a positive quality of life for each contributing team member.*

Remember that it is called a mission statement, not a mission essay. Concise mission statements are more memorable and effective.

Mitsubishi Electric, U.S. Cooling & Heating

Mitsubishi Electric, U.S. Cooling & Heating will continually improve its technologies and services by applying creativity to all aspects of its business. By doing so, we enhance the quality of life in our society, pioneering customized comfort, together, until every room in every building is comfortable.

Harker Heating & Cooling, Inc.

It is the intent of Harker Heating & Cooling, Inc. to provide a quality product, installation, and excellent service to our customers at a fair and competitive price, by maintaining a safe and financially secure work environment for our employees.

See the Appendix for a video link on Tony's *Best Year Ever* series.

12.
Utilize the Power
of Visualization

*"Create a vision board for your company that represents your goals
and accomplishments. It is very motivating."*

High achievers get results because they know what they want and
they execute a plan to get it. But before they do any execution, they
visualize the result.

Successful people create a tangible vision that motivates them toward
what they desire to achieve. They
understand how important it is to
engage the visual aspect of motivating
themselves and their teams toward
their goals. Visualization is a key
aspect of becoming a winner and
achieving exactly what you want.

**VISUALIZATION IS A KEY
ASPECT OF BECOMING
A WINNER AND
ACHIEVING EXACTLY
WHAT YOU WANT.**

Remember that clarity pulls you
toward the outcome and the results
you envision. There is a pulling power
to clarity that guides entrepreneurs
to achieve their dreams and goals. But it is not enough to just have a
goal. Ridiculously successful people are very clear and specific about
their goals. How? They utilize visualization techniques.

One technique is to create a vision board of your business goals. Cut
out photos of what you want and post them for you to see daily. This
continual reminder is a powerful trigger. Another technique is to create
a list of what you want more of and less of in life (get MOLO template
with free kit; see back pages of book for additional details).

Both of us have used powerful visualization in our lives for decades by seeing the goal we want before it's achieved. For years, I (Tony) have helped people improve their thinking and use tools to create mastery in their lives and businesses. I have a vision wall that I look at daily, with inspiring images of goals and also goals I've attained. This vision wall includes pictures of family vacations, my kids' events, and business achievements. I

> VISUALIZATION IS THE ABILITY TO "SEE" THE END RESULT BEFORE YOU BEGIN.
> –PETER THOMAS

encourage you to start practicing the power of visualization today by taking several hours to create images of the goals you want to achieve. (Google Tony Jeary on "Results Boarding" for a powerful video on the topic.)

When I (Peter) started selling mutual funds many years ago, I was reading a business magazine and in it was a picture of a Lear Jet. It was the most beautiful thing I had ever seen, and I knew in my heart that I wanted one. I cut the picture out of the magazine and put it up on the wall directly across from my desk. Six years later, I actually owned that jet.

The power of visualization is one of the most powerful motivating tools you will ever have. What are the things you are visualizing into reality? Get clear on what you want to have, share, and most importantly what you want to become—as it relates to both your personal life and your business.

Benchmark HVAC Vision Board

In a world full of distractions, we need constant triggers and visual markers to keep us on track and focused, similar to how highways have signs that mark the right way to your destination.

13.
Document Your Preferences with Pictures and Video

Create and post clear and non-assuming pictures, videos, and documents as instructional tools for company practices, processes, and standards. This can be extremely valuable for both new and existing employees.

Some of the best "how to" instructions can be given in the form of pictures and videos. With today's technology, you can take photos from your phone to demonstrate the right ways to do things.

The same is true for demonstrations with videos. A short video can even be sent to your teams via text message or email and can demonstrate great sales tips and techniques, the proper installation proce-

dures of a product, or a reminder of specific performance standards or processes.

If you want your team to really understand what's expected of them and you want to help them be their best, don't leave things to chance. Show them what you want. Post photos; provide diagrams; and, when possible, share a demonstration with a short video. This will also create consistency for your brand. Consider having a few things that are unique to you that will differentiate you and your brand from others, and be sure that everyone knows what is expected.

Help your team live up to your expectations, and everybody wins—the customer gets great products and service, the employees are equipped to do their job, and you will continue to build a solid, reputable brand in the market.

14.
Plan Your Week Utilizing White Boards

"Draw out your daily goals so you and your people can easily see them. Also lay out your weekly, monthly, and annual plans."

USING A WHITE BOARD PROVIDES VISIBILITY, ACCESSIBILITY, AND FLEXIBILITY; AND IT FOSTERS CREATIVITY.

It is often helpful for your team to see a snapshot of what is going on as a whole in order to better understand how they fit into the picture. Post white boards (white 4 x 8 sheets of shower board) and use as dry erase boards for planning your week (service, appointments, installs, sales calls). It will also help when managing the flow to ensure all the pieces fit together and commitments are met. It is a great way to track progress where everyone can see, and progress is inspiring to your team.

In addition, consider adding your daily goals to the boards, as well as weekly, monthly, and annual plans, along with your mission statement. Use different colors for emphasis. This creates a sense of clarity for every person on where you're going and how you're going to get there.

Where appropriate, post successes so that everyone can see and share. Leave a space for others to give ideas or ask questions if possible.

Using white boards is a great way to create simple diagrams or mind maps that have relevance to the team for sharing installation techniques or solving consistent problems.

15.
Go as Far as You Can See

*People oftentimes don't act until they can fully
see an entire solution. For maximum results,
go as far as you can see, and then you can see farther.*

A major premise embedded in *Strategic Acceleration* is to go as far as you can see, and then you can see farther. I know you remember when it was reasonable to consider your plans and strategies on a five-year basis. A traditional question you have heard many times is "Where do you want to be in five years?" That question is now somewhat obsolete because of the speed of life. A more relevant question today is "Where do you want to be next week?" That's a bit extreme, but that's what it feels like sometimes. You can plan only as far as you can see. That is the point.

For example, during my work with George Burke, I asked him what he thought about clarity and how his understanding of clarity had changed. Based on his own experiences, George said he thinks everyone has things in their belief window that limit what they believe they can accomplish. When George achieved the limit of what he thought he could do, there was a feeling of "now what?" that settled over his life—and when that happened, he lost clarity. He believes his own lack of clarity became evident when he reached whatever success ceiling he had imposed on himself by his own beliefs. Therefore, to maintain clarity, it demanded that he purge those self-imposed beliefs regularly.

I certainly agree with George, and *Strategic Acceleration* optimally requires an annual purging, at a minimum. George gained clarity when he had a perfect blueprint of what he needed to do and accomplish for the next twelve months. This blueprint enabled him to predict exactly where his business would be at the end of the twelve months.

To create that kind of blueprint, you have to think deeply about all you do and why you do it. Then you have to transition the results of your thinking into action to gain new experience. New experience is required to be able to see farther, which is also what you have to do to climb the Effectiveness Ladder.

A Clarity Blueprint includes the following key components:

- What you want to do
- Why you want to do it
- How you will do it
- The benefit of doing it
- The negative result of not doing it

When you know all these things, you will achieve clarity and you will be clear about what you really want.

TIME

16.
Say "No" Often

Maximize your time as well as your people's time
by saying no to all or part of things that aren't important.
Negotiate for less time when you can.

In today's fast-paced world, we are presented with opportunities almost every waking minute. Services, messages, products, emails, phone calls, offers, meetings, and activities bombard us on a continual basis. We are possibilities people, so sometimes these things look attractive. But it is possible to have too many choices. Say no to the things that don't matter the most. That's the magical rule. It takes discipline and good thinking to a whole different level.

> **WHEN YOU SAY YES, YOU'RE SAYING NO TO SOMETHING ELSE.**

People don't say no because they don't know how, they don't want to miss out on anything, or they don't want to offend someone. But people-pleasers are rarely wildly successful entrepreneurs. If you don't learn how to say no, needless activities can pile up on the calendar, draining valuable moments from important projects and goals—valuable moments from your life that you'll never get back.

So many people say yes and get into messes, partnerships, deals, and relationships because they didn't say no at the right time. Most often the right time to say no is at the beginning.

Say no strategically. There are a lot of ways to say no and make people feel as if you still care. If you're an author, for instance, you can say no to a free speech opportunity and offer to send them a free case of your books for their group or event. If you're an entrepreneur who gets invited to participate in a deal, you can say no and send one of your colleagues to the meeting instead and to do the research.

Saying no can also allow you to offer an alternative. Instead of saying yes to a meeting for an hour, say no; then suggest meeting for fifteen minutes instead. Remember that you're maximizing your time and your people's time as well.

When you say yes, you're saying no to something else. When you say yes to a client dinner, for instance, you could be saying no to dinner with your children. When you say yes to counseling someone after work, you could be saying no to counseling a family member in your own home. When you say yes to lunch with a friend, you might be saying no to an important deadline getting completed at the office. If you say yes to every activity, meeting, lunch, or volunteer opportunity, you're saying no to anything else that could have been in that time slot. It is easier to build relationships and build your business when you eliminate so many of the distractions, unwanted attention, unnecessary obligations, and meaningless meetings.

> TAKE TIME FOR REFLECTION, INTROSPECTION, AND STILLNESS. TAKE THE TIME TO BLOCK OUT THE WORLD AND BE WITH YOURSELF.
> –PETER THOMAS

Saying no is empowering. It helps build your self-esteem, reduces stress, and gives you more time and energy. Successful businesses are not built on a feeling of obligation or a fear of saying no. Successful businesses are built when clarity, focus, and execution converge over and over again.

Saying "no" to your LLAs (Low Leverage Activities) also creates space. In order to create margin time, which is that extra space in your life that you very rarely have, you have to start getting good at saying no more often. Even if it's just a moment of solitude, the time you create is better than engaging in something you didn't want to be a part of in the first place.

17.
Manage Time (Don't Let Time Manage You)

"We all have the same amount of time. Be aware of how you invest yours and ensure you are doing things that are in keeping with your priorities."

When it comes to business, winning, and defeating the competition, we need to realize that everyone has the same amount of time to begin with. How we utilize that time can make the difference in winning and losing. Do you value your time? And will you use it to build a competitive advantage?

Avoid time and energy wasters—those distractions and people that suck both time and joy right out of your day. Detox your life from anyone who isn't good for you, or wastes your time, distracting you from your goals. A lack of discipline and poor habits are indicators of a lack of success, and unsuccessful people don't want the other person to win. Often, these people are time wasters with a lot to say; and if you allow them to, they will talk incessantly about their problems, their lack of business, or the conflict that they're having with friends or family. Before you know it, you've missed a deadline or an important business meeting, or you've given up hours that could have been spent on something valuable.

> **THERE ARE 168 HOURS IN A WEEK. YOU SLEEP 56 AND DO MAINTENANCE FOR 12; THAT LEAVES 100 HOURS. MANAGE THOSE HOURS WELL!**
> **–TONY JEARY**

Managing time also means managing your emotions. I (Peter) have found over the years that I am very active and very alert, with my radar always on. In several instances, this has proved not to be good, especially at airports. I used to get very caught up in some of the ridiculous situations that occur when taking a flight. After a particularly bad experience in some international location where our bags were lost and no one seemed to care, I decided to learn a way to de-stress myself and gracefully cope with whatever issues come up, rather than getting so worked up that it ruined my day and affected the moods of those traveling with me.

I took a self-hypnosis course from Dr. Lee Pulos, a friend and a fantastic teacher. He taught me how to take myself "down" so I invented what I called my Zone One, Zone Two, and Zone Three. These Zones represented levels of activity and emotion. Zone One was fully alert and highly sensitive—my normal condition; Zone Two was slowed down considerably, more observant than reactive; and Zone Three was almost comatose.

> THE KEY TO GOOD TIME MANAGEMENT AND EMOTIONAL HEALTH IS TO BE PROACTIVE, NOT REACTIVE.

I decided that I would let my wife handle all logistics and I would go into Zone Three as soon as I got into the airport. It has worked perfectly! It has been a long time since I have let an airport stress me out, and I guarantee you that my wife and travel companions appreciate this as well.

What you do with your time matters. People can either multiply your time or waste it. They can accelerate your emotions or soothe them. The key to good time management and emotional health is to be proactive, not reactive.

Time management in today's fast paced world is and must be at the very top of the list of critical functions your business masters. Why are other companies out-performing your company—do they get more hours in the day? No, they make better use of their time and maximize it.

Be aware of where you invest your time and keep your priorities in line with your time management.

18.
MOLO Your Life and Business (More Of, Less Of)

*"Constantly audit yourself and your business.
What should you be doing more of or less of?"*

What do you want more of in life? In business? In your relationships? What do you want less of?

Most people look at conducting a MOLO (more of, less of) exercise as something you do for an entity, or for an organization, not an individual. But being able to utilize this as a leadership tool allows you to ensure you're detecting where your opportunities truly are, and that you are capitalizing on your strengths, efforts, time, and resources.

Make lists for what you want more of, and what you want less of. MOLO forces you to continually think of what you want to keep and what you want to eliminate, much like the vision (results) boarding exercise (see #12). Consider posting lists in a visible place in your house and office so that you see them every day. Keep MOLO in the forefront of your mind. Focus on the things you want more of like health, deals, fun clients, or other business contacts so they will be drawn into your world. The more focus, the more draw. The things you want less of will help you best route energies elsewhere.

> **FOCUS ON THE THINGS YOU WANT MORE OF SO THEY WILL BE DRAWN INTO YOUR WORLD.**

Get rid of the things you don't want in your business and life. Get rid of things that complicate and clutter. Many know what they want more of, but few strategically think much on eliminating things like excess meetings, recourse debt, toxic people, or even things like conflict.

We say eliminate every negative, if you can. Suppose someone gave you an object you loathe, and you feel irritated—even just for a second—each time you see it. Sure, it's only one second or two, and you feel obligated to keep the item; but over the course of a year, that's a lot of seconds that bring you negative feelings. Why would you keep it? This is a small example of a big principle. Don't say yes when you mean no, and don't live with things you don't like. Don't allow things in your business that drag morale down, pull happiness away, or even just cause undue stress.

If you focus on eliminating friction every day, you will dramatically impact your life. What do you want to stop doing, start doing, or do differently? Audit yourself, your team, your whole organization, and determine what you need to do more of, less of, do differently, start doing or stop doing. This rule is one of the most impactful things I've (Tony) coached Peter on and he shares this knowledge with all those around him.

You can even use the MOLO exercise for constant improvements within your team. Do this exercise in team meetings, asking each person to make a list of things they want more of and less of. This group brainstorm session will help you determine how to improve and how to save time.

> **NO ONE HAS ENOUGH TIME, YET EVERYONE HAS ALL THERE IS. WHAT WE DO WITH OUR TIME DETERMINES WHAT WE ACCOMPLISH WITH OUR LIVES.**
> **–TONY JEARY**

The MOLO Matrix is available to download free in in Mitsubishi Electric Contractor Toolkit.

www.mitsubishipro.com/toolkit

19.
Create "Elegant Solutions"

Combine activities to accomplish multiple tasks at once (i.e., train someone at the same time you are talking to a customer). Doing two or three things at once can be powerful. Ask yourself, "What can I do at the same time and still do it well?"'

> AN *ELEGANT SOLUTION* IS BEING SO CLEAR ON YOUR GOALS, OBJECTIVES, AND PRIORITIES THAT YOU CAN DO ONE THING AND ACCOMPLISH MULTIPLE OBJECTIVES AT THE SAME TIME.
>
> –TONY JEARY

An *Elegant Solution* is when you are so clear on your objectives that you can accomplish more than one thing at a time by combining them. It's a powerful way of prioritizing and maximizing your time.

Ask yourself if you're really clear on your vision, where you're going, and what your goals and objectives are. Are your goals and objectives in front of you where you can be reminded of them every day? When you have clairty, you will continually think of ways to create Elegant Solutions and accomplish several objectives at one time.

One example of an Elegant Solution that I (Tony) really like is to have fitness-based meetings. For clients who have the same goal of maintaining physical fitness as I do, I invite them over to my gym to work out, talk, and generate ideas on a flipchart. One positive outcome is that that two-hour block of time is spent in the gym working out. Another outcome is that I can talk about business with my clients. Another positive result of that Elegant Solution is that a staff member or colleague is taking notes, interjecting ideas, or capturing what's going on. Elegant Solutions create wins for everyone involved.

Another example would be providing personal and business value to your clients at the same time or conducting more efficient meetings. Consider taking a valued client or colleague out for a day of golf where you have an opportunity to show appreciation on a personal level, but at the same time you solidify relationships and have a chance throughout the day to discuss business opportunities as well.

In order to maximize my time, I've had a driver for twenty years who drives me to meetings so I can do business in the backseat, take notes, read, and conduct conference calls—all because I don't have to drive.

> CREATING *ELEGANT SOLUTIONS* LEADS TO MULTIPLE WINS.

Examples of Elegant Solutions:
- Invite someone you're mentoring (or perhaps a new team member) to participate in a meeting that would simultaneously add value to and teach him or her.
- Take your kids on a business trip with you to help them learn and spend time together while you're working.
- Plan a business lunch or happy hour at a popular networking spot to perhaps connect with others at the same time.
- Select places to vacation where your family can learn a new culture or experience something new, while also spending quality time together. Talk about your goals on the trip.
- Host an event that both brings value to your clients but also connects them with others who can bring value to them.
- Work out with a business colleague or client.

This is a heightened level of thinking that can bring amazing results. Ask yourself, "What actions can I do at the same time and still do each well?"

Creating Elegant Solutions leads to multiple wins. What you do with your time determines what you do with your life. Begin to rethink your time habits and better understand how the time investment choices you make really affect the results you seek. Then, work to create elegant solutions that allow you to accomplish more in the same amount of time.

20.
Understand Positive and Negative Procrastination

"First understand that everyone procrastinates. It is not always bad. Be smart when you delay, and don't delay when you shouldn't."

Let's face it—we all procrastinate sometimes. But you can't produce results until you start doing something. There are two kinds of procrastination: positive and negative. Positive procrastination can be beneficial, whereas negative procrastination just impedes production and therefore results. An example of positive procrastination is when you legitimately need some "mental percolation" time to gather your thoughts. Negative procrastination is based on a flimsy excuse to avoid doing something now.

Production Before Perfection (PBP) is the self-talk that says it doesn't have to be perfect to get it going; get it going and perfect it along the way. It's my solution to negative procrastination. Let me repeat—you can't produce results until you start doing something, right? If you do nothing, that is exactly what you'll get—nothing. If you do something, the possibilities are endless.

Just a warning: When you start to practice PBP, you will be doing

> LIVE *PRODUCTION BEFORE PERFECTION* (PBP). THE MAIN IDEA OF IS TO ACT FIRST, AND GET IT PERFECT LATER. OPERATING WITH A PBP MINDSET HELPS US FLOW MUCH MORE EFFECTIVELY IN THE FAST-PACED WORLD WE LIVE IN TODAY.
> –TONY JEARY

things in a way that conflicts with the thinking of 90 percent of people on this planet, so be ready to encounter resistance. It is not the natural thing to do, and you will have to hear and overcome objections on why you should wait. But waiting and getting results are not compatible. If you wait, you burn time you cannot get back. The same goes for your team and your entire organization.

People who use planning to avoid action often get tangled in an unhealthy emotional cycle of evaluation and analysis paralysis. Preparation and planning are important, but excessive preparation is nothing more than procrastination—it's that simple. It is only when you start doing what you need to do that you can begin to produce results.

Sometimes the best way to manage your emotions is to ignore them and keep pushing through to achieve what it is you need to do. If you procrastinate, it means you are fearful of failure and may not be confident in your ability to succeed. This is when the words you say to yourself (self-talk) become extremely important.

People who quit too easily or give up in the face of adversity generate a complex chain of emotions and events that negatively impact their mind, hence their business results. It is always easy to quit, and too many people prefer quitting to the discomfort they experience when the going gets tough. The reason is simple: Adversity is painful. When you quit in the face of adversity, it means you are deficient in the mental substance it takes to persevere and overcome. Go as far as you can see, and then you'll see farther. This concept has the power to nip procrastination in the bud before it has a chance to flower.

You don't always have to understand all the details between where you are and where you want to be. Instead, be realistic and be strategic. You simply have to forge ahead, despite any resistance or desire to procrastinate. Your success is right around the corner.

> **WHEN YOU QUIT IN THE FACE OF ADVERSITY, IT MEANS YOU ARE DEFICIENT IN THE MENTAL SUBSTANCE IT TAKES TO PERSEVERE AND OVERCOME.**

21.
Delegate a Lot More

Delegate many things that can free up your load of LLA (Low Leverage Activities), so you can focus on HLA (High Leverage Activities).

The magic of delegating is getting things done faster, period! When you delegate smartly, you're often creating space for the High Leverage Activities (HLAs), those things that matter the most.

A good sign that you need to delegate more is if you are continually tired, overstressed, overworked, and unhealthy. If you don't have time to work out or if you're constantly rushing from one place to another, chances are you need to delegate more small things to make space for the big things. Think intelligently about your life and manage time more wisely. It's the foundation to reaching a higher level.

The best way to look at delegation is to examine your goals and activities and identify which things absolutely cannot be delegated. Lunch with a client, for instance, is something that perhaps only you can do. However, sending an email to a prospect might be something that your sales person or assistant could do instead. Be creative—if you hired a college intern during peak times, what administrative tasks could that person help you with?

Building relationships shouldn't be delegated, but administrative tasks are a perfect example of things that

> AN ESSENTIAL FUNCTION OF LEADERSHIP IS TO PERSUADE AND MOTIVATE OTHERS TO PURSUE EXCELLENCE BY HELPING THEM BECOME WILLING TO EXCEED EXPECTATIONS.
>
> –TONY JEARY

can be delegated effectively. Just make sure you're not doing anything that somebody else can do better. Perhaps someone on your team is really great at bookkeeping, billing, collections, or marketing and social media. If you delegated those things, what could that free you to do?

Once you start strategically delegating, it can become addictive and you'll want to delegate more, because it will give you more time and energy to focus on the things that you enjoy and are good at doing. Be careful not to micromanage once you delegate and negate the process. Your relationships can become stronger and your business offers will often increase as a result. Your effectiveness as a leader—in fact, your whole world—can change.

22.
Measure Everything, Including How You Spend Your Time

If you want your time to be better spent, then understand where you are spending it by actually being keenly aware and measuring it. Challenge yourself to take one or more areas of your life or business that could use improvement, figure out what measurements matter to you, and then assess, measure, and adjust accordingly.

If you really want to perform as a leader at the top level, or in any other area of your life, you need written targets and you need to measure progress against those targets. In order for top performers to be their very best, they can start with a simple assessment centered around leadership best practices to create real focus and results that matter. Assessments can measure leadership ability, time management, meeting effectiveness, or any other objective.

It might seem like an extra step to measure everything, but it will save time and money in the long run. Measure install times, service call times, and other things that are key to your business, and set them as standards. Develop expectations of completion based on these standards. Create incentives for those who consistently meet or exceed the standards—that's one great way to get your team members on board with time management. You can also reward people for finding ways to shorten the process without cutting the quality of the work and share those best practices with the team.

If you want to improve your health, maybe you'd measure your BMI, blood pressure, or waistline. Leadership skills could be measured by how well you strategically plan, prioritize, or deploy your team. You might want to improve your financial position, so you'd examine bank balances, P&Ls, investment worksheets, or other critical success factors.

Take a few minutes and jot down where you are and where you want to be. Get your team involved; your family involved. See for yourself how much measurement matters! Real measurement over and over means real results and will bring a whole new level of focus on measuring and refining.

Measure not only what is successful or unsuccessful, but measure to know how the good can be better. The smallest detail could make the difference in your P&L and in your life.

Since it can be great motivation to have visuals of your goals, build charts on the wall; use templates to fill in times and expectations. If you want your time to be better—measure it so you'll know how and where you can improve.

23.
Leverage Technology to Improve Everything

Keep up with and use the latest technology to save time. Put your lists on your phone and use your tablet for demonstrations.

Virtually every person in business today carries a mobile phone. Even with all the great technology we have at our fingertips today, we often underutilize the tools we have right in our hands—our phones and tablets are effective communication tools that truly maximize efforts to get better results. Further, using modern-day technology eliminates coordinating phone calls and emails, which can save huge amounts of time.

Here are just a few considerations for better leveraging today's technology for greater efficiency:

USING TECHNOLOGY AS A STRATEGIC ADVANTAGE CAN CREATE A WIDE VARIETY OF EFFICIENCIES, SAVE TIME, AND STREAMLINE EFFORTS.

- Have all project managers sync calendars and task lists with their teams and others for better time management across the organization.
- Provide employees the ability to text or chat with each other on smartphone apps.
- Automate with a personal touch. Make it feel like the interface or interaction is designed especially for that one customer.
- Have sites for that specific segment you want to sell with demos on tablets for each person on your sales team.
- Track all information and history of customer interactions.

- Utilize your notes app to keep your "To Do" list or other critical information relevant to your day.
- Send out inspirational phone or text blasts daily or challenges that inspire your team.

Chances are, you are already spending dollars to have the latest technology available for yourself and various team members. Using technology as a strategic advantage can create a wide variety of efficiencies, save time, and streamline efforts.

24.
Pre-make Installation Kits For Selected Jobs Prior to Install

"Prepackage certain items in advance to take to the job site. Being proactively prepared and super organized is a powerful time saver."

How many times have you or your crew arrived at a customer location, begun the project, and realized you don't have everything you need? You have to leave and make a trip to the supply house, which is unproductive and unbillable time. You get back to  the location and start again, only to find something else is missing.

Having pre-made kits available—such as ductless, furnace, AC, and RTU kits—will save time and money, allow you to be better prepared and organized, and help the installers be more efficient on the job. It allows you to know exactly what you have spent on the job and also saves the time to gather everything individually. It also saves time by just going to one place to pick up all your items.

Whether you utilize the 'bundling' services of your local distributor or you prepare job material bundles in your own shop, you reduce, if not eliminate altogether, the number of trips made to the supply house. In addition, the project goes in faster, there is less materials waste, and your install crews can be more efficient and productive.

Lists are available to download free in Mitsubishi Contractor Toolkit. www.mitsubishipro.com/toolkit

25.
Improve Your Organizational Skills

Every organizational improvement you make will have an effect on the bottom line of your life and, in effect, give you more time!

Personal disorganization is a tremendous waste of time. Being schedule-oriented does not necessarily guarantee organization. *To improve your organizational skills, you need to have a plan that complements both your schedule and personality.*

Here are five questions that directly affect your level of organization.
1. Is your workplace functional and arranged properly?
2. Is your desk (briefcase) organized by using folders or organized piles to keep future work away from current work?
3. Do you utilize office supplies and organizational supplies correctly?
4. Do you use a planning tool?
5. Is your filing system efficient and usable?

Many people find it hard to step back from their work and see what needs to change about their organizational habits. If you take time to get organized, you'll gain time in the long run. *Just as it takes money to make money, it takes time to gain time.* Every organizational improvement you make will have an effect on the bottom line of your life... more time! Focus on your top priority tasks every day before working on less urgent tasks.

After you improve your organizational skills, it is unlikely you will ever return to your previous level of disorganization. The systems you initiate should suit your needs so precisely that once you get comfortable using them, you will be happy to maintain them.

There are so many other exciting things to do in life than shuffle paper, react to hourly crises, and increase your stress level. Don't wait until it's too late; take time to get organized now. If you don't feel like you have time to get organized, then you are a prime candidate for improving your organizational skills.

Write down your workspace needs by asking yourself these questions:
- How can my drawers be set with supplies to save me time?
- How can I arrange my workspace for brochures, forms, or reference books?
- How can I create a large open surface for layout of paperwork?

Clean house regularly. The "Toss or Keep" test is one way to determine whether or not you should keep something or toss it. Here is the simple test:
- Have you used this item within the past year?
- Is it serving a specific purpose?
- Do you have a place to store it where you can find it again?
- Can you replace it easily if you need it?

Early in your quest for an organized office, it is important to determine where everything will go. Studies have shown the most successful and productive people have a clean desk.

An ideal way to decide what should and shouldn't be on top of your desk is to ask yourself the following questions:
- Which items do I use every day?
- Which items do I use at least once a week?
- Which items do I use less than once a month?
- Are there any items—probably decorative—that I never use?

To win the paper battle, put your papers to the "Paper Test." The more papers you throw out, the fewer you will have to deal with.
- Will I ever refer to this piece of paper again? If *No*, toss it.
- Will I be able to replace this paper later if I discover I need it after all? If *Yes*, toss it.
- Would I jeopardize my job or business if I threw it away? If *No*, toss it.

When it comes to paper, the motto is "simplify, simplify, simplify!" Here is a helpful acronym for dealing with paper.

- Put it in a stacking bin (with a Post It Note™ describing the next action)
- Act on it
- Put it in a file
- Enter it on your to-do list and file it
- Rid yourself of it

26.
Hold Effective Meetings

A leader's culture is strongly influenced by how effective meetings are for communicating, strategizing and synergizing.

What if your organization could...
• Reduce time spent in meetings by 20 percent or more?
• Get back precious time wasted on inefficient handling of email?
• Increase productivity by implementing a strategic, clear, focused approach to meetings and emails?
• Cultivate a culture that encourages preparation, clear communications and rigorous follow-up?

Know that meeting effectiveness is a must for high-performing teams. The ability to lead efficient and effective meetings can be a major contributor to your professional credibility, image, and success.

Holding effective meetings is part of the culture that is managed by the top leadership. What strong leaders do, others model. Inefficient meetings are a tremendous time-waster—and wasting time is not a habit of an effective leader. A leader's culture is strongly influenced by how effective meetings are.

This includes ensuring all meeting invitations have a why, and that the actual meetings themselves have strong objectives. Also important is developing a clear agenda tied to those objectives, as is ensuring the right people are in the right room for the right amount of time. Finally, clear actions should end each meeting. Meeting Effectiveness means people want to come to your meetings versus avoiding them.

Well-executed meetings enable people to show up prepared, efficiently absorb the intended message, address issues at hand, and immediately get to work executing the right things.

Meeting Standards

1. Have a clear purpose and defined objective(s) for every meeting.
2. Ensure that the right people are either in the room, on the phone, or represented.
3. Create and follow a realistic, timed agenda.
4. Start and end meetings on time.
5. Acknowledge that achieving winning outcomes is not just the meeting leader's responsibility, but everyone's responsibility.
6. Facilitate for results so that everyone stays involved and engaged.
7. Take thorough notes, documenting important discussion points, outcomes, and agreements.
8. Develop a "who does what by when" action plan.
9. Publish meeting notes and action plans quickly, and follow up to ensure timely execution.
10. Strategically cascade meeting outcomes promptly and consistently to others in the organization.

STRATEGIC

27.
Be Intentional About Everything

Balance your time between tactical (calls/paperwork/cleanup) and strategic (thinking/visioning/planning) to get even better results. Too often, leaders focus too much on the day-to-day things and not enough on the planning.

> WHEN YOU ARE IN TUNE WITH YOUR VALUES AND YOU KNOW THE VALUES YOU LIVE BY, YOU BECOME INTENTIONAL ABOUT EVERY ASPECT OF YOUR LIFE.

> BE BOTH STRATEGIC AND INTENTIONAL ABOUT EVERY SINGLE THING YOU DO.
> –TONY JEARY

Intentionality is different than clarity or focus. Intentionality comes from the root of your intention. It centers not just around thought, but also action. Be intentional about who you spend time with. Hang around others who match your values. Be intentional about every action.

It all starts with clarity (see #8). When you are in tune with your values and you know the values you live by, you become intentional about every aspect of your life. In business, you should have set standards for what you want and what you don't want, well thought out and documented. If a big part of your success is the people around you, then replace those who aren't right for you with some who are.

Tactical vs. Strategic

What is Tactical?

- Tasks
- Calls
- Activities
- Paper Work

What is Strategic?

- Planning
- Thinking
- Studying

Most People Need to Be More Strategic

Be intentional about how much stress you can manage, how many projects you can take on, and why. Don't do things without thinking. Think. Be strategic, then do things fast and your energy and resources will be expended and utilized in the best way.

What we value in ourselves and what others appreciate about us often relate to our self-esteem. Take time to identify the qualities and characteristics you like about yourself—your natural talents and strengths. When you take time to think about and identify your values, you become much more intentional.

Intentionality exists when you know exactly what you want, and everything flows from that. First, you must know what you really want. Then you can be intentional about taking action.

What's Your Strategic IQ?

- What percentage of the time do you (and your team) operate in the tactical?
- What percentage of the time do you (and your team) operate in the strategic?

DO YOU HAVE THE RIGHT PRINCIPLES ON YOUR *BELIEF WINDOW* RELATED TO THIS RATIO?

28.
Use Tools That Give You Leverage

"Buy, lease, borrow, or create tools that help both you and your people save time. Be more focused and consistent. Measure, be accountable, and get results."

Having the right tools at the right time can make a world of difference.

Most people don't really understand that if they have an arsenal of tools, they'll execute faster. Most people work harder and put their own internal team under more stress because they're constantly meeting, sending out sales emails, trying to get prospective buyers, and responding to leads. But you don't have to be like most people.

When you have tools, you already have the response ready. You are taking a proactive approach. Tools can help you sell, raise money, and manage and lead people. You don't have to recreate the wheel to buy, lease, or attract a big toolbox.

> **HAVING THE RIGHT TOOLS AT THE RIGHT TIME CAN MAKE A WORLD OF DIFFERENCE.**

Create an arsenal you can send to clients as well. In our office, we create books, DVDs, book recaps, and even goal setting or business plan templates that we give away to clients to help them win. We give people tools that will help them succeed at business, team building, development, or strategy. When they win, we win.

As a leader, you should have a big toolbox for your organization. If you don't know where to start to create your toolbox, make a list of the things people want from you. Instead of recreating the wheel, develop a tool mindset. Do you need an app? Do you need a book? What tools do your competitors have that you don't?

To be more valuable as an entrepreneur or as any kind of leader, we recommend you build an arsenal of tools you can use to provide value to others and to help you present your messaging. That means setting up a system, both for yourself and your team, that you can use to catalog and organize items of value and content, and build your own research toolbox.

An arsenal can be in the form of a list of helpful URLs or videos, powerful books, summaries, whitepapers, examples, case studies, photographs, animations, and more. Just like a military arsenal, the idea is to "arm" you in your business to respond quickly. The real concept is that little by little, week by week, month by month, you're building an intentional arsenal. That arsenal can sometimes be leveraged down. You can even have others maintain it for you.

Utilizing an Internet site where appropriate is one way to utilize your arsenal. The key is that it becomes more powerful based on the friendliness and retrievability of the content. The more robust your arsenal, the better equipped you will be to respond to every situation.

29.
Ask Questions and Learn

Continually be looking to get best practices from others;
learn best practices from other contractors and from your
TMs to leverage for the whole team. Be curious.
Always be willing to entertain new ways and ideas.

Asking a question creates automatic engagement with another person or an audience of people. You can be much more resourceful, powerful, and productive in life if you learn to ask questions to get specific answers.

Have you ever had a conversation with someone who only answered in two- or three-word sentences, and you walked away feeling like you learned very little or hardly had an encounter at all? They might not have been intentionally giving you short answers. Perhaps you could have phrased your questions better.

A lot of people fail to understand the power of asking good questions.

WHEN WE ASK GOOD QUESTIONS WE ARE MORE LIKELY TO GET RESPONSES WORTH LISTENING TO.

People often move into talking and telling instead of stepping back, asking about priorities, and listening. You'll never know what's on their mind, what's working, what you can help them with, and what's going well in their world if you don't ask.

One effective tip for asking stronger questions is to frame your questions in a positive tone. For example, instead of asking, "Hey, what's been going on with you lately?" ask, "Hey, what are the best things going on in your life right now?" Framing things positively assures the direction of the conversation and creates a memory peg with good feelings from the conversation. Remember: Ask questions so the customer talks, and listen so the customer's needs are satisfied.

Just as it is important to ask the right questions of customers, it is important to keep yourself at your peak of effectiveness by asking yourself questions like, "What matters most to me?" "What's the best use of my time right now?" "What do I do the best?"

When it comes to business, ask questions that help on a practical level. TMs see a lot of contractors; ask them to bring you strategic ideas that will help your business. Capture the best ideas from all of your industry sources and then implement!

30.
Turn the Numbers Into Action

"Consistently set aside time—weekly, monthly, and quarterly—to think about and analyze metrics and adjust your plan accordingly."

In specialized trade industries such as contracting, a lot of business owners have created success from originally being great at their trade, not necessarily being business-minded from the start. Yet, to sustain continued growth and solidify a strong foundation, taking the time to step back and evaluate all the metrics can be significant for uncovering cost-saving practices and leveraging best practices that bring high yields.

CAPITALIZE ON SUCCESSES BY REPEATING WHAT'S WORKING.

When you take the time to review your data, you may be surprised at how telling the numbers are, even in one specific area. Look for opportunities to cut costs or do things differently that will create a higher yield. You never know where you may have Blind Spots that if discovered, could create additional profits.

Focus on high-material jobs that have less labor. Look at your most profitable jobs and determine the material-to-labor ratio, and then go after more of those types of jobs. If the ratio is close to 1–1, stay away from it or raise your gross margin for the job drastically.

The best way to create continued success is to know what brought you success in the first place—specifically, and in detail. Let the numbers and metrics tell a story, and then capitalize on the successes by repeating what's working.

31.
Utilize and Learn From a Mystery Shopper

"To be on top of your game, have select people check out your performance—how your phone is being answered, how your techs are doing with customers, how complaints are being handled."

I think everyone would agree that, to be successful, you strive for a high level of customer satisfaction with your products and service. You also want to get the best return on the investment you're making in people, communications, material, and time. But, do you really know how your customers perceive your brand based on their individual experiences? Is your team creating great experiences that result in loyal customers or are they sending them to your competitors?

Hiring a mystery shopping company can give you great insight into the answer of those questions. The real benefit is that it provides first-hand data relating to those "moments of truth" (i.e., how individual customers rate their experience). From this data, you have the ability to provide better training, adjust performance, and identify areas of needed improvement.

UTILIZE A MYSTERY SHOPPER TO CALL YOUR ORGANIZATION TO STANDARDIZE A HIGH LEVEL OF CUSTOMER SERVICE.

The most successful programs are those linked to reward and recognition. Let your people know that you utilize this service, that your purpose is to catch them doing something *right*, and that they will be rewarded for outstanding feedback.

Mystery shopping works for multiple areas of your operations—sales staff, office staff, technicians, and more. Every touch point provides an opportunity for a customer to consciously choose you.

32.
Build Set Pricing

"Building a set price for your services helps eliminate price negotiations, better positions you to spiff the service technicians' handing over the leads based upon equipment and type sold, and often creates higher margin tickets."

Being prepared matters—it's also a best practice for Mitsubishi Electric, U.S. Cooling & Heating. There's great leverage in being able to sit down with a consumer, asking the right questions, and being able to offer a price right then and there.

As Rob Rickman says, "This matters because we live in an 'I want it now' kind of world where we can find out anything about anything by going online. People don't want to wait days or weeks to get a proposal on how much a Mitsubishi Electric, U.S. Cooling & Heating, ductless system will cost them. They want the price now."

Having the pricing available up front is a matter of sitting down and learning how to price a job up with the tools that are available—and it is usually developed over time with some mistakes along the way. There are several tools you can use, like the Harshaw method of how to price a job.

The initial calculations will take some time and effort but once done can easily be modified when needed. This helps Mitsubishi Electric, U.S. Cooling & Heating by showing the consumer that our network of dealers is professional and ready to make the sale. It also gives you credibility in the consumer's eyes when you have all the available information they might need up front.

33.
Utilize Preferred Customer Agreements

Preferred Customer Agreements create a trust and value between you and your customer base when they know they are serviced as a "priority" over regular customers. It also ensures you stay in front of that customer at least twice a year, giving you the opportunity to upsell and ask for referrals.

One of the most frustrating things a customer has to endure when any type of service is needed is the "wait." While most good contractors are going to have pretty full schedules already, the Preferred Customer Agreement is a way to generate revenue and also provide extra value to your customers and make them feel special.

While each person's agreement will be somewhat different, benefits can include points like:

- Maximized efficiency with scheduled tune-ups of listed equipment included (preventive maintenance)
- No overtime charges on service calls
- No diagnostic or trip charges for service calls
- Reduced repair costs with discounted parts and labor
- Priority customer status
- Supplemental heat, if needed
- Same-day service (if called prior to noon on day of service)

The customer is also then virtually guaranteed to remain your customer because they have an agreement. It allows you regular access to them and a better understanding of their needs to also recommend other products and services, as well as ask for referrals.

Consider providing incentives or rewards for each Preferred Customer

Agreement sold to increase the number of sales.

The Preferred Customer Agreement is available to download free in Mitsubishi Contractor Toolkit.
www.mitsubishipro.com/toolkit

34.
Include Warranties

Guarantee the equipment you install. This comforts your customer and helps alleviate buyer's remorse, possibly adding to a higher close rate and a higher margin ticket.

Oftentimes people believe that giving a product guarantee will trigger a loss of money by customers wanting to find a way to make a claim. In reality, it removes the risk factor in making a big purchase decision for the buyer and gives them confidence that you are the right vendor to trust if you are willing to back up your product in writing.

Give a one-year money-back guarantee on the equipment you install. This comforts your customer and helps in alleviating buyer's remorse, possibly adding to a higher close rate and a higher margin ticket.

Providing a guarantee says to the customer that you, too, have a standard that must be met; and that if for some reason there is a problem, you will replace it or fix it at no cost to them. In the end, it will gain long-term customer loyalty.

Here are some great examples Richard Harshaw uses for "Service Agreements/Sample Strong Promises."

Consider the following as service option guarantees:
- If you call for service and we are not at your home within six hours, we will pay you $50 on the spot.
- If you call for service and we cannot get your system running properly by dinnertime, we will place your family in a (good quality) hotel overnight and buy your meals until we can get your home back to a safe and comfortable condition.
- If you ever become dissatisfied with our service, you may cancel at any time. We will cheerfully refund your full purchase price, and pay for your next service call from a contractor of your choice.

FOCUS

35.
Understand and Study the Concept of HLAs

Determine what your true High Leverage Activities (HLAs) are. These are the 4–8 activities that, when done consistently, provide the most amount of value for your time and provide the biggest return. They're not always what you think.

What we do with our time determines what we do with our lives, and is a direct reflection on our success. Everyone agrees that time is valuable, time is limited, and we should maximize it. But most people have not clearly developed a mental system for leveraging the best use of it.

NO ONE HAS ENOUGH TIME, YET EVERYONE HAS ALL THERE IS. BE A RIVER, NOT A RESERVOIR.

You want 70–80 percent of your 100-plus available hours per week directed toward the High-Leverage Activities (HLAs). These are the activities that can give you more impact and accomplish multiple objectives at the same time, both personally and professionally.

What are your HLAs? I challenge you to do what I have done and write them down in your smart phone so they are at your fingertips at all times. I have a set of HLAs for both my personal life and my professional life.

Most people are amazed by the time that can be gained simply by being more organized and focused. Knowing and working in your HLA zone will keep you organized. When you are really organized, your life can flow like a river. Opportunities flow to you and through you because you've made it a goal.

And it doesn't just work for you personally. Talk with your team and mutually discuss what each person's HLAs are. Print them out, discuss them often, and measure the results this change in focus can achieve.

Ask yourself, what's the best use of my time *right now*?

1. **Filter your actions** accordingly, and take action based on what will give you the highest leverage for your time.
2. **Say "No" to the right things.** People will pull and tug at your time all throughout the day. Learning to say "no" to the right things allows you to be more productive and stay focused.
3. **Thinking can be a Blind Spot.** A lot of people don't look at HLAs as *thinking*. Know how to think both strategically and tactically to get the best results.
4. **Manage delayed gratification.** In today's fast-paced world, we want everything now. We are all about accelerating processes. We also understand the value in planting seeds that will grow. There is a balance.
5. **Help others win.** Helping others win has a multiplying effect, and it creates a desire for those people to help you win.
6. **Listen your way to success.** Be interested, not just interesting. Stop waiting for your moment to speak.

> KNOW YOUR PRIORITIES AND FOCUS ON THEM. IT IS ONE THING TO DO THINGS MORE EFFICIENTLY, BUT ARE YOU ACTUALLY DOING THE RIGHT THINGS?

7. **Leverage lists.** Sounds simple, right? Most people form a habit of keeping things in their head. I propose for maximum results, you write out your lists. Then keep them wherever you are, including on your smart phones or tablets.
8. **Develop Systems that Keep Paying.** Systems can help you be your best and create habits that help you get accelerated results!

36.
Focus—the Opposite of Distraction

Often, the difference between someone who is successful and someone who isn't is extreme focus. What you invest in is what will grow. You really do get more of what you focus on.

If you focus on your relationship, you'll have a good one. If you invest in your business, you'll have a good one. Invest time, resources, and energy in your business, marriage, and kids, and those things will grow.

In today's ultra-competitive world, getting superior results faster is critical to success—and so many people want it! However, this hectic speed of life makes it easy to become sidetracked by things that steal priority and make us less effective. Before long you've lost focus and don't even know it until your business or a relationship begins to suffer.

We've seen many entrepreneurs operate in "overwhelmed" mode. They become mired in the daily activities, unable to get off the hamster wheel of meetings and reactionary emails, calls, and activities, and then they lose focus. The business goals begin to drift farther and farther away.

> SUCCESSFUL ENTREPRENEURS MUST HAVE EXTREME FOCUS.

Successful entrepreneurs must have extreme focus. It's easy to get pulled away from our goals by people, places, ideas, or things. Every material thing you own requires time and energy. Every new purchase, every idea, and every new person who enters your office or day requires attention. It takes an intentionally focused person to minimize distractions. And focus is the opposite of distraction and is critical to high achievers.

The first three chapters in Tony's book, *Strategic Acceleration*, describe the importance of developing clarity about your vision, as well as understanding the "why" behind it. A clear and authentic vision enables willing changes in behavior and sets you up for success. Gaining clarity on your vision, however, is just the first step in the *Strategic Acceleration* process. The second step—focus—will teach you how to better develop this important skill.

I (Peter) have all kinds of tricks to get myself focused and diffuse distractions. Once when I was facing several difficult business challenges simultaneously, I went out and purchased a GI Camouflage Helmet and presented it to my lawyer. I told him we would be going to war and I needed him to be thinking 24/7 of ways to win the war. Losing the war was not acceptable by any standard. He placed the helmet in his office in a very prominent place. I wanted him to be thinking of solving my problems all the time. It worked! We won the war.

> FOCUS IS A THINKING SKILL ACQUIRED AS A RESULT OF MENTAL DISCIPLINE.
> –TONY JEARY

If you ever find yourself in need of setting short-term objectives, get a physical item as a visual image to keep your team focused, so they never forget how important their support is to you. The reason there are winners and losers is because usually the losers lose their focus and are not totally and completely absorbed with the success of the objectives.

Once you have the ability to focus on your vision (and all of the strategies, tactics, and actions required for its success), you will be ready for the final step—execution—and you will act on and accomplish your vision results faster.

37.
Aim for 87 Percent

Don't allow your standards and commitment to mastery to interfere with getting things done; 87 percent is often good enough.

There's a saying that goes, "Excellence adds value; perfection just adds time." So many people are out for perfection to such a degree that they either stop because they can never reach their desired state, or they put in significantly more time than there is value for the last few percent.

> ### DON'T ALLOW YOUR STANDARDS AND COMMITMENT TO MASTERY TO INTERFERE WITH GETTING THINGS DONE; 87 PERCENT IS OFTEN GOOD ENOUGH. BE OKAY WITH IT SOMETIMES AND MOVE ON.
> –PETER THOMAS

I (Peter) have a concept I call the Rule of 87 Percent. You will be amazed at the results if you quit being a perfectionist and understand that as a rule, 87 percent is just fine. Do you want to be known for value? Do you want to be known for excellence? Absolutely. Oftentimes, excellence comes in at 87 percent. Striving for perfection will sidetrack your results and make your customers wait. They want results, and they want them fast.

When you're negotiating a deal or engaging in any kind of business proposition, don't lose sight of what's important. Focus on production and the critical factors in the project. Focus on your highest-leveraged items and activities; and when you hit 87 percent success, celebrate!

Why not 100 percent? Because in all our years of experience

> IF YOU'RE CONTINUALLY FOCUSED ON ACHIEVING 100 PERCENT, YOU'LL BE CONTINUALLY DISAPPOINTED, ESPECIALLY WHERE OTHER PEOPLE ARE INVOLVED.

in coaching and living in the entrepreneurial world, we've seen analysis paralysis and the stress of focusing on perfection cause people to lose more than they win. If you're continually focused on achieving 100 percent, you'll be continually disappointed, especially where other people are involved.

High expectations are great, but there are always other factors in any situation. In most cases, 87 percent will be just as good as 100, or better because of the worrying, stress, and negative energy that come with trying to achieve a perfect score.

This also aligns with the ready, fire, aim model which encourages to not get caught in "analysis paralysis" syndrome. Plan what you want to do, and then take action and GO. You can always adjust after you have started. Remember, even if you are on the right track, you will get run over by our competition if you just sit there!

38.
Focus on the Right Priorities

The most common obstacle with HVAC contractors is not a lack of motivation, ability or intelligence. It is not a lack of desire or willingness to do the work that needs to be done to be successful. It is a lack of focusing on the right priorities.

One of the oldest axioms in management is that "it's not enough to do things right; you must also do the right things." This requires the ability to focus on the right priorities—otherwise we risk making progress in the wrong direction in our lives and businesses.

Steve Jobs said that one of his mantras was "focus and simplicity." Likewise, one of the keys to success in the residential HVAC business is focusing on simple things; nevertheless, this is more difficult than it may appear at first blush with the countless distractions that bombard us every day.

With all the never-ending distractions, what exactly should we focus on? This question simplifies itself when you distill life into its three basic areas: money, relationships, and health. When you think about it, what else is there? Your money is your business or your profession; your relationships are your family and friends; and your health is your physical, mental and spiritual wellness.

The key to success is to target specific desired results in each area. In his classic book, *Think and Grow Rich*, Napoleon Hill taught us to have a "definite purpose" if we want to create wealth and prosperity in our lives. Sounds a lot like focus, doesn't it?

With that in mind, think about one goal in each of those areas and be specific. Identify a "definite" income or business goal, a definite relationship goal, and a definite health goal. For example, perhaps a specific goal in each area might be to earn $200,000 per year, to be an awesome spouse and parent, and to lose twenty pounds.

Then, to further simplify things, identify just one or two things that, done on a consistent basis, would likely lead to the desired goal. The key here again is to keep it simple. Success is not about the scope of your actions; it is about the consistency of your actions. It's about finding little things and repeating them over and over.

To illustrate, consider focusing on "running every call with passion and purpose" and "diagnosing every homeowner's comfort and efficiency problem and recommending solutions to every problem." If you did just those two things on every call, what is the probability that your income would dramatically increase? Pretty good, I would say. It's pretty simple, too.

> IF TODAY WERE THE LAST DAY OF YOUR LIFE, WOULD YOU WANT TO DO WHAT YOU'RE ABOUT TO DO TODAY?

Want a better marriage? Try telling your wife she is beautiful and amazing every morning and never raise your voice to her. Pretty powerful, and yet incredibly simple.

Want to lose twenty pounds? Try reaching for a second serving of salad instead of dessert and hitting the gym a few times a week. If you did that, what are the odds you'd hit your weight loss goal?

The key to success in life is focusing on a few simple things you want and a few simple things you need to do to get the things you want. Don't overcomplicate it. The confused mind says "no" and becomes paralyzed. Keep it simple and stay focused on the right priorities.

Perhaps Steve Jobs said it best, "If today were the last day of your life, would YOU want to do what you're about to do today?" Your time on earth is limited; don't wait! Make it count, and prioritize all that you do to create the business and life you want.

39.
Maintain Control of the Sales and Installation Processes

To increase revenue and profitability over the long haul,
you must elevate the importance of the sales function and
approach sales from a systematic perspective.

Imagine that you arrive at the site of a new residential installation. After you greet the homeowner, he says to you, "I am really excited about our new system. Now here is how I want you to do the installation..." And from that point on the homeowner tells you step-by-step how to do your installation. What would you say to that homeowner? Or at least, what would you *want* to say to that homeowner?

In all likelihood, you would never allow the homeowner to run your installation. If you did, there is a good chance the system would never run properly. After all, the homeowner knows nothing about installing an HVAC system.

Because you value consistently delivering quality installation results for your customers, it is necessary that you maintain control over the installation process. You must protect the integrity of your process. No matter how good the homeowner's intentions, any meddling can only diminish the quality of your installations.

The same is true when it comes to consistently delivering high performance sales results. If you want to deliver quality sales results, you must maintain control over the process; nevertheless, on sales calls we sometimes allow the homeowner to run the sales process. And we do this to our own demise.

You wouldn't allow your homeowners to run your installs; and if you want to maintain consistent results in sales, you can't allow your homeowners to run your sales calls. If you allow homeowners to run your sales calls, no two sales calls will be presented the same. Each homeowner wants something different. Some may want a price first; others may want you to inspect their existing equipment first.

If your sales activities are random, it's certain that your sales results will likewise be random. Random sales activities produce random sales results. Consistent sales activities produce consistent sales results.

So if your sales are sometimes good and sometimes bad, they are by definition "random." Most likely, your random sales results are the result of allowing the homeowner to run your sales process.

If you are frustrated by inconsistent sales results, the only cure is approaching the sales function from a systematic basis. This requires making a commitment to elevating the importance of the sales function in your business and investing in a simple and reliable sales system. Consistent sales activities produce consistent sales results.

Contributed by Weldon Long, who is author of the New York Times *bestseller* The Power of Consistency *and the creator of The HVAC Sales Academy. For more information visit www.HVACSalesAcademy.com.*

40.
Set Specific Goals to Grow Your Ductless Business

Setting specific goals also sets expectations. People are motivated by goals; and when they know what is expected, most will strive to achieve, and hopefully exceed, those goals. Then, habits are formed.

Develop a laser-like focus on what works. Ductless works. Decide to focus on ductless, and your efforts and business objectives very well might exceed your expectations.

I (Tony) remember a conversation I had after a seminar with a guy named Mike with NETR, who wanted to drastically increase his systems sales by 50 percent. This is one of our biggest contractors in the country.

Having goals helps to get the contractor in the right mindset. But by writing down and tracking goals, companies are more likely to hit targets. When a contractor sets a goal to sell 50 or 100 systems per year, now they know they need to sell 1 to 2 systems per week. This helps keep them focused and on target.

> **DEVELOP A LASER-LIKE FOCUS ON WHAT WORKS. DUCTLESS WORKS.**

The majority of contractors who do not sell a lot of ductless systems view ductless as just another offering. The most successful contractors in the industry have decided that they want to grow this segment of their business. They realize that ductless systems are more profitable per man-hour. The more systems they sell, the more they are installing higher profit jobs.

Once contractors have made the decision to focus on ductless, then they start making decisions that promote the sales of ductless heat pumps. Specifically, they start to spend money on marketing ductless.

Analyze the profitability of your business. Look at the job costing of different types of jobs. Figure out for yourself that ductless is more profitable. Many times contractors intuitively know that it is more profitable, but they have never put pen to paper to document it for themselves. Once you do that, you can set specific goals that will help your business grow.

For a download of the complete Mitsubishi Electric Difference brochure, go to www.mitsubisihipro.com/toolkit.

BRAND, MARKETING & SALES

41.
Ensure Strategic Alignment Between Your Branding, Marketing, and Sales

Know your customer reach (i.e., one hour away). Make sure your branding is thoughtful and that your marketing tools all match, making your sales efforts easier and more effective.

In many companies, what you have are silos of individuals in each of the different areas of branding, marketing, and sales. In fact, sometimes you even have different department heads who aren't always working in unison like they could. If this happens, step back and make sure you are really clear on the branding message that you want to be communicating.

From a marketing perspective, all of the marketing tools in your arsenal should be congruent with your branding message so that you have the power of instant recognition —that sameness, if you will—that comes with using the same colors, the same thinking, the same words, and the same methodology. Think about your web presence, videos, brochures, PowerPoints, handouts, and leave-behinds. Having that alignment can bring business in and make sales a slam-dunk. (In the Appendix is a marketing tool audit to help you really look at your marketing efforts/tools in an efficient way.)

We've seen many times that people in the sales arena pull from the marketing arsenal, and it's not always consistent with the brand.

> ALL OF THE MARKETING TOOLS IN YOUR MARKETING ARSENAL SHOULD BE CONGRUENT WITH YOUR BRANDING MESSAGE.

That alignment can be a huge deal. Make a commitment today that in every organization you start, run, manage, or lead, you will ensure all three of these important areas—branding, marketing, and sales—are strategically aligned.

This model is available to download free in Mitsubishi Contractor Toolkit.

www.mitsubishipro.com/toolkit

42.
Build Your Brand

Branding is one of the most powerful ways to grow your business. When customers think of HVAC/R, you want them to think of and recognize you. Be consistent in how you present yourself to the world and in your marketing with logos, imaging, and attire.

Branding is the number one way to grow your business. When your customers think HVAC/R you want them thinking of you, but how do you do that? You do it by building your brand.

A great way to build your brand is by marketing through direct mail, radio, newspaper ads, and social media. The most important thing to remember when using those types of marketing is that you must consistently be building your brand. Tell your story, what makes you the best, and what you are offering that no one else is offering.

All of your ads should look a certain way, and they should be consistent with the message you are trying to portray. If you want people to think about energy efficiency, then your ads should talk about energy efficiency and how you bring that to your customer.

Here is an example; A contractor in Maine wrapped its vans, sent out direct mail pieces, and ran radio and television ads that all showed the same imaging. It was a very simple marketing scheme, but it worked because that contractor's brand had consistent marketing.

Build your brand and be consistent!

The sky is the limit as to what can be done today by wrapping vehicles and using billboards and other cost-effective marketing options.

Anything you can do to build your brand that gains visibility and ties back to you as a contractor will help attain a higher level of consumer awareness.

43.
Make Sure Your Employees Are an Extension of Your Company Brand

How your employees present themselves is an extension of how your company is perceived. Have standards and consider uniforms (especially shirts and caps).

Your employees are an extension of your brand, good or bad, and putting standards in place can help ensure they are a positive extension.

There are many ways an employee will be an extension of your brand. One way is that they are a visual representation. Many companies provide shirts and caps to create a unified look and to duplicate the visual brand of the company that can be seen on their websites, trucks, business cards, and other visual marketing. It can also make customers feel more confident that the person providing service is a legitimate representative of your company.

It is important to have standards to ensure employees are neat and clean and that their clothing has no rips or tears. Many people recommend having extra shirts available in case a job gets extra dirty and there is a need to change clothes midday.

Your employees are more than a visual representation of your brand. Make sure they know what you stand for and what your mission is so they can also represent you verbally in the most positive light. At a minimum, the standards for your employees should include being polite, not swearing, and not using the homeowner's toilet.

Consider coming up with some key phrases for use in responding to customers. A good example is the response used by the employees of The Ritz Carlton, a company known for its commitment to exceptional service. Whenever you say, "Thank you," to a staff member who has helped you or served you, their response (with a smile) is "It is my pleasure." It is a small thing, but words have power; and those gestures go a long way in differentiating yourself from your competitors.

Build a culture that supports people treating the company as if it were their own, and where there is pride in representing your strong, positive brand.

Any use of the Mitsubishi Electric corporate logo on vehicles must be authorized by Mitsubishi Electric US, Inc.

44.
Be the Local Authority

*"Being known for a winning brand like Mitsubishi
can give great pull to your company name."*

What are you known for? You don't have to be good at everything, but you should be excellent in at least one area. Find that one thing and be the expert. Know your God-given talents.

I (Tony) get results. My clients and prospects know that I help them get what they want faster, and that I am a true "encourager." I (Peter) am a deal maker, and I've been very successful at it. I had a vision for making Century 21 Canada a success when no one else believed in it, and I did. I sold the company for many millions.

Whatever you are good at, be known for it, and consistently excel in that field. Understand what's driving that success and identify any areas that are holding you back.

If you don't feel like you're good at any one particular thing, ask yourself why. You may already be very successful. On the other hand, you may have struggled with achievement and may not be as successful as you would like. Whichever the case, it may be a good idea to look at the choices you have made and the principles governing those choices. Regardless of your current achievement level, you can always improve. Get clear on your strengths; know yourself well. Leverage your strengths and talents.

> YOU REALLY DO GET MORE OF WHAT YOU FOCUS ON—FOCUS ON THINGS THAT SUPPORT YOUR GOALS AND VISION.
> –TONY JEARY

If you want to gain notoriety, make friends with the media and be

BEING KNOWN FOR A WINNING BRAND LIKE MITSUBISHI ELECTRIC CAN GIVE YOU GREAT PULL.

their go-to expert source concerning HVAC and comfort. Set up interviews with home and garden magazines and companies when the cooling or heating season begins.

Sign up as a vendor in local home improvement shows or similar events and hand out cards, product pamphlets with factual data, customer testimonials, etc.

Check out opportunities to be a regular columnist in local newspapers or online blogs. Participate in TV spots where possible to position yourself as an expert.

Connect with your local hardware store and host an HVAC pro-day at their location, and have your expert staff on hand to demonstrate and answer questions.

Dominate your area with targeted mailings to neighborhoods of your recent installations, and use testimonials.

The more visible you are, the more people will begin to associate you with being the local expert. Be everywhere, and have a professional presence.

45.
Do Favors in Advance (FIA)

*Doing favors in advance for your customers, your people,
and your potential customers creates a sense of loyalty and
a feeling of reciprocation.*

INSTEAD OF DOING FAVORS BECAUSE YOU EXPECT SOMETHING IN RETURN, DEVELOP AN ATTITUDE OF PAYING IT FORWARD AND GIVING VALUE IN ADVANCE.

Remember the last time someone did something nice and unexpected for you? Maybe they sent you a gift or referred you to a new client, or perhaps they performed a task to help you out so that you didn't have to do it. Favors in advance are favors that you do for people regardless of your status with them, or desired outcome. Instead of doing favors because you expect something in return, develop an attitude of paying it forward and giving value in advance.

We have seen numerous people over the years who are hesitant to do for others, unless that individual is going to pay off in business or do something for them. But that thinking is just wrong. Do things to help others. Think of the people who are in your inner circle in business, and continually do favors for them. Will you extend your database and share your connections? Live in abundance versus scarcity.

This rule works for strangers as well as clients, friends, and prospects. People like to do business with people who do things for them and who work to build a platform of trust. Why not be a giver?

We both like to give things away. Whether it's a book, a LifePilot binder, or something else that can enhance another person's life, we've found it helpful to have tools on hand to give to others. Tony has them in the trunk of his car and carries resources in his briefcase for chance meetings. Have a bookshelf of giveaways. It's about being prepared with an arsenal of information so you can do favors in advance. Help people win, and be generous.

Building a bank account of favors done in advance is a form of valuable social capital. People want to help those who have helped them, so look for ways to give others what they want. Take the time to ask about these wants and needs, and document them in a way that makes it easy for you to follow through.

> SOCIAL CAPITAL BUILDS CREDIBILITY TO REQUEST FAVORS AND ACTIONS FROM OTHERS.

This social capital can dramatically impact your power!

"Results in Advance" demonstrate your ability to perform by doing something small for free.

46.
Networking Will Add Value

Join associations, organizations, and peer networking groups where you can gain valuable best practices, insights, and mutually beneficial connections to help your customers get what they want. Networking and connecting others is a powerful way to add value.

Being a person who connects the dots is valuable and powerful, because you make things happen. Being a connector is a way to bring unforeseen value to other people, as well as to yourself. It's really natural for some, and others need to put thinking power to this concept. It is about influence. Every entrepreneur and leader needs the leverage and knowledge that others provide. No one can do it alone.

If you like people, connect them. They win and you win. I (Tony) have 25,000 people in my contact database, and I use these connections to help my clients connect and grow. Do you have a system for creating a database from your business cards and connections? What does that system look like?

One industry group that provides a wide array of networking opportunities is Nexstar Network®. Nearly 500 members benefit from sharing experiences and insight with each other. Their members build relationships by helping each other, thinking together, and incorporating what others have already tested, proven, and implemented through peer group meetings, regional networking groups, and numerous other networking events

> TAKE ADVANTAGE OF THE WEALTH OF KNOWLEDGE, INFORMATION, AND SUCCESS ALREADY OUT THERE JUST READY FOR THE TAKING TO TAKE YOUR BUSINESS TO THE NEXT LEVEL.

built around meetings and training programs.

Leverage the opportunity to utilize your network with your manufacturers. If you don't already know about the offerings, ask them.

Consider becoming a Mitsubishi Electric Diamond Contractor and participate in one of the peer group best practice meetings, as well. Peer groups from noncompetitive regions freely discuss financials, growth strategies, and mutual threats and opportunities on a regularly scheduled basis. Also consider location association meetings where you may gain valuable insights from successful business people in other industries that translate back to your own business.

> LOOK FOR WAYS TO CREATE WINS BY CONNECTING PEOPLE WITH OTHERS WHO HAVE THE KNOWLEDGE AND EXPERTISE TO HELP THEM GET THE RESULTS THEY WANT.

Take advantage of the wealth of knowledge, information, and success already out there just ready for the taking to take your business to the next level. Continually expand your network, because you will need the help of others to accelerate your achievement, and it helps to be on a first-name basis with your important people.

You can learn more about Nexstar Network® at www.nexstarnetwork.com.

47.
Be "Presentation Ready"

Be prepared always. Make sure each team member and each vehicle is armed with marketing materials or tablets so your company is always presenting and selling the very best way.

As an entrepreneur, there are always people investing in you, and there are almost always strategic partnership opportunities. Being presentation ready for each customer can often make or break an opportunity.

You should continuously be presentation ready, so when the phone call comes in from a potential client, you're ready to give them prices; if you meet someone at an event, or if an unexpected meeting comes up, you can pull from your arsenal.

> HAVE A CATALOG OF PROJECTS WITH PICTURES TO SHOW CUSTOMERS, INCLUDING NOTES ON THE CHALLENGES AND THE SOLUTION THEY PROVIDED FOR THE PROJECT.
> – PEDRO CARRES

A person's *Presentation Universe* is pretty large and expands well beyond just the "big presentations." Life is a series of presentations, and being ready for each opportunity is a great asset to have in your corner. Do an inventory of all the potential types of presentations you may need to give: a 30-second elevator speech; a two-minute conversation; a formal presentation; a staff meeting; and talks for recruiting, customers, and investors. Outline some key points for each of these talks and practice them. The more ready you are in advance for each of these opportunities, the more likely you'll walk away with your desired outcome.

Most owners and architects, and some engineers, have a tendency to think that VRF air-conditioning technology is too new. They don't feel comfortable with the idea of being guinea pigs with their buildings. When they ask contractors how many Mitsubishi Electric VRF jobs they've done, more often than not the contractors will mention a few jobs they've installed here and there.

WIRELESSLY CONTROL HOME COMFORT FROM ANY PLACE, AT ANY TIME

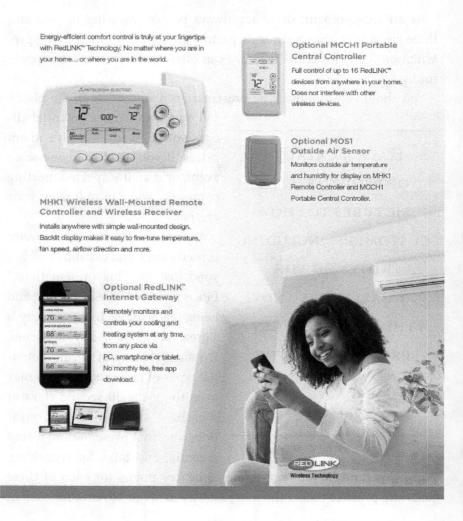

Energy-efficient comfort control is truly at your fingertips with RedLINK™ Technology. No matter where you are in your home... or where you are in the world.

Optional MCCH1 Portable Central Controller

Full control of up to 16 RedLINK™ devices from anywhere in your home. Does not interfere with other wireless devices.

Optional MOS1 Outside Air Sensor

Monitors outside air temperature and humidity for display on MHK1 Remote Controller and MCCH1 Portable Central Controller.

MHK1 Wireless Wall-Mounted Remote Controller and Wireless Receiver

Installs anywhere with simple wall-mounted design. Backlit display makes it easy to fine-tune temperature, fan speed, airflow direction and more.

Optional RedLINK™ Internet Gateway

Remotely monitors and controls your cooling and heating system at any time, from any place via PC, smartphone or tablet. No monthly fee, free app download.

REDLINK
Wireless Technology

A more convincing response would be for the contractor to show their prospective customers a catalog of VRF projects they've completed, including pictures, a description of the work done, and the solution they provided. This marketing material proves very effective when explaining your track record of projects with this technology.

LIFE IS A SERIES OF PRESENTATIONS, AND BEING READY FOR EACH OPPORTUNITY IS A GREAT ASSET TO HAVE IN YOUR CORNER.

Each of your team members should have presentation material in each vehicle. Put an HVAC system in your office and set it up as a demo. Continually provide a sales toolkit with updated material and presentations, and practice those presentations in the office to get feedback.

48.
Generate Leads—Become A Marketing Machine

Devote a certain percent of your gross revenue to marketing efforts (7–12 percent is recommended) to keep the phone ringing; and, of course, be sure and ask for referrals. Your happiest customers will help create others.

Look at marketing as an investment and not an expense. Marketing typically drives revenue, rather than the reverse.

Put an annual marketing plan in place; then review it quarterly for results and adjust as needed. Michael Cappucio's "Market Your Company" worksheet recommends the following elements to include in your marketing plan:

> **LOOK AT MARKETING AS AN INVESTMENT AND NOT AN EXPENSE. MARKETING TYPICALLY DRIVES REVENUE, RATHER THAN THE REVERSE.**

- Set up plan annually on how you are going to market your company.
- Set up budgets based on previous year's sales.
- Review previous years' marketing plan for its successes vs. failures to improve the new year's plan.
- Track your leads.
- Set up monthly budgets. Plan each month.

Additional ways to generate leads and become a marketing machine include:

- Leverage manufacturers to get leads. They get them all the time; and if you aren't getting leads, you should be asking for them.
- Because the majority of people search for new vendors on their smart phones and tablets, it is important to have a mobile friendly site. Consumers are more likely to buy from a mobile-friendly site. The highest performing category comes from website, web pages and social networking.
- Using pay-per-click with keywords relevant to your market can generate an enormous amount of leads, as well, and brings you to the top when people search for their heating and cooling needs.

49.
Minimize Risk.
Grow Your Sales.

Minimizing or eliminating the risk for buyers in making a purchasing decision greatly increases the probability of a sale.

There are many things buyers evaluate when making a purchasing decision, but none of them is more important than risk. When you understand the impact of risk, you can tailor your sales process to minimize or even eliminate it and help drive yours sales through the roof.

The calculation is very simple: the lower the risk of making a purchasing decision, the easier it is for the prospect to say "yes." The higher the risk of making a purchasing decision, the more difficult it is for the prospect to say "yes."

Therefore, when the risk is high consumers search for any way they can to minimize it. It may manifest itself as wanting better warrantees or a better price or a better company. But however it shows up, it's all about minimizing the risk of making the wrong purchasing decision.

Imagine you are going to spend a significant portion of your hard-earned money on a new HVAC System for your home. What are the consequences of making the wrong purchasing decision? How high is the risk? It's very high, isn't it? If you choose the wrong HVAC company, you could lose a lot of money, couldn't you?

Of course you could. So what do you do? You negotiate a lower price to effectively lower the risk. You get three bids. You postpone the high-risk decision. You think, think, and think, about the various options. This is a big decision, and the risk of making the wrong purchasing decision is very high.

But imagine if there was no risk in the purchasing decision. That would make the decision to purchase much easier, wouldn't it? The lower the risk, the easier it is to say "yes."

Retailers, of course, have known this for many years and have minimized risk for their customers by offering liberal return policies. If a consumer is standing in the aisle contemplating the purchase of a new pair of jeans, they are more likely to say "yes" if they know that they can return the jeans if they get home and decide they don't like them. There is no risk in making the wrong purchasing decision, so it's easier to say "yes."

We all expect to be able to return a hammer to The Home Depot, a television to Sears, or a pair of jeans to Walmart; but what about other products and services such as new HVAC Systems that are not traditionally offered with a "risk-reversal" guarantee?

Risk-reversal guarantees and risk-minimizing guarantees are powerful ways to dramatically increase sales. Many HVAC companies have been offering this type of guarantee for many years with significant success. Rarely does a homeowner actually want a full refund; they simply want their system to operate correctly.

Minimize the risk and watch your sales skyrocket. It works for retailers and it works for hundreds of successful HVAC contractors.

Contributed by Weldon Long, who is author of the New York Times *bestseller* The Power of Consistency *and the creator of The HVAC Sales Academy. For more information visit www.HVACSalesAcademy.com.*

50.
Use Videos for Marketing and Sales

Use a video to showcase your best projects, and then promote it to consumers to credentialize your work.

A residential customer can gain trust in your work and the product by seeing a quick professional video.

You don't have to create the content yourself. Leverage from the manufacturer, distributors, and local marketplace to create a video library, because much of that information already exists. If you aren't aware of these tools, just ask. Search out any and all opportunities to build off of the already-existing video arsenal available to you.

Videos don't always have to be professionally made. With smartphone technology, many contractors will get an on-site testimonial when a technician leaves the jobsite. The video doesn't have to be professional; it simply has to convey the message that the job was done right and the customer is happy.

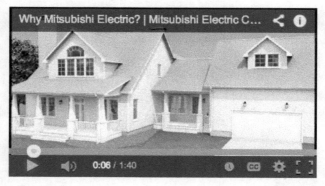

For samples, go to www.youtube.com/user/MitsubishiHVAC or visit our user submitted video site at www.youtube.com/playlist?list=PLBD332BD57F199D1D.

51.
Make a Binder of Residential Jobs

Create a branded binder of photos and testimonials for each vehicle to provide social proof in gaining customers.

When making major purchases, homeowners want to be confident they are making a well-informed decision with a reputable company. One way to validate your reputation and expertise is to create a visual representation of your jobs with photos, testimonials, and installations to show the customer during an in-home sales call. Photos of installations ensure consistent representation of your work and are a great tool that allows sales people to engage with the customer.

The visual helps show the homeowner that the contractor is organized, trustworthy, and efficient. The testimonials provide third-party validation of satisfied customers. People want to do what other people do, and this provides social proof that they are making a good choice. They can also be used to help overcome objections, since others have testified to the quality of the products and services.

The same effect can be accomplished with the use of a tablet, as well. Both tools serve to show the customer that you're professional, you've been around, you do quality work, and you can be trusted.

Make it easy for your customer to decide to do business with you.

52.
Differentiate Yourself from the Competition

Helping customers differentiate between you and your competition is often critical to getting a sale. Focus on selling customized comfort.

When you ask people what makes their company different from their competition, it is amazing that many will answer with things like, "our people," "we've been in business for a long time," "we have the best products," etc. If everyone says those are the things that make them different, then, in essence, they are all the same.

So, how do you really differentiate yourself from the competition? And what is your Unique Selling Proposition (USP)? A unique selling proposition is *what your business stands for*. It's what sets your business apart from others because it's *what your business takes a stand about*. Instead of attempting to be known for everything, businesses with a unique selling proposition

> A UNIQUE SELLING PROPOSITION IS *WHAT YOUR BUSINESS STANDS FOR*. IT'S WHAT SETS YOUR BUSINESS APART FROM OTHERS, BECAUSE IT'S WHAT YOUR BUSINESS STANDS FOR.

stand for something specific, and it becomes what you're known for.

Many businesses make the mistake of attempting to stand for everything when they first get started. They want to do everything well, and they want to be all things to all people. They want to be known for having the highest quality products AND the lowest prices. The problem is, when you attempt to be known for everything, you don't become known for anything.

Ask yourself, "If I were the customer, what would be in it for me to do business with me"? If you don't have a good answer, then chances are customers won't be compelled to buy from you over someone else.

Many contractors lose sight of the fact that they are selling comfort above all else. With Mitsubishi, the contractor is selling the ability to create customizable comfort. This needs to be the heart of the conversation.

In addition to the other questions you normally ask, consider asking how they use their home. What are their living trends and personal preferences? Does the homeowner have an area they need to use as flex space, such as a workout room or man cave that cannot account for variable loads? Do they need more living space, such as a conditioned garage? These should all be items discussed in the home.

By the end of the in-home conversation, the homeowner should understand that you are truly different than your competitors, as you are offering a level of customized comfort they have not experienced before. This will help differentiate you in your market as well.

Make customers aware of what you offer.

53.
Utilize Social Media

A great majority of people are now on social media.
This is a free tool to create a visible online brand.

Social media can be a powerful, free way to market your company and get visibility. If you don't have a social media presence, there are some pretty compelling reasons why you should. Here are some stats of four of the top social media sites in the world: Instagram has 200 million users; Twitter is now at 225 million; LinkedIn is up to 300 million; and Facebook is the largest social media site in the world, with 1.28 billion users.

A great example of how to utilize social media as a contractor is to view what Hoffmann Brothers Heating & Air Conditioning, based out of St. Louis, have done with their Facebook page. All in one site, a potential customer can go and see a wide variety of postings that allow them to view the things that are the most important to them.

Under the Photos section, there is third-party validation with high

recommendations from Angie's list; the cover of a magazine in which their company was featured; coupons with valuable savings; staff photos; and even photos of their trucks out in the field, with their logos everywhere on the site.

In the Postings area, there is a variety of heating and cooling tips for consumers, testimonials, job postings, and other miscellaneous items that make for an interesting and informative site.

They use their Facebook page for two reasons: 1) to promote business services, and 2) to blog about the large commercial projects they are working on at the time. By asking their followers questions that may specifically relate to their business, they can connect with them as though it were a conversation. For example, see the blog posted about workplace carbon monoxide (CO) poisoning. They point out things that the typical employer would not know about his/her building, and suggest ways that they can help by listing their credentials in the same place.

Other blogs deal with energy conservation, which has helped them get business through government-related entities that can sponsor some of the events they put on and to refer their business to others.

We recommend you create a Facebook page that you can refer others to; then invite your friends, family, and customers to "like" your site and share their experiences. Show the quality of work you can provide and show the level of experience you have. This will add trust to the homeowner.

54.
Follow Up with Every New Customer

"Immediate follow-up allows you to ensure the customer had a great experience and to ask for referrals, which are the best way to grow any HVAC business. Ongoing follow-up reminds your customers to think of you, and even refer you, for all their HVAC needs."

Once a sale is made, even when contractors are reputable and do an exceptional job, they often fail to use the follow-up as a strategic tool. Referrals are the best way to grow any HVAC business, particularly for ductless. For a product that is still considered cutting edge, getting a referral from a client is invaluable. People who have ductless love it. Once our contractors have created raving fans, then they can't help but tell their friends and family.

Customer follow-up serves multiple purposes, and each plays an important part in gaining a customer for life. It is important to talk with your customers first and foremost to make sure they were satisfied with the service they received. If they were, the follow-up will remind them of their pleasant experience yet again. If there were any problems, the fact that you called to follow up will allow you to remedy whatever issue there may be, which will be appreciated by the customer and put you back in a positive light.

Once you know you have a happy customer, ask for referrals or references. Ask them to write you a letter or email, or even to post about their experience on your social media page. Send them an email with a link asking them to "like" or subscribe to your social media pages to get great energy savings tips throughout the year and even seasonal discounts on products and services.

Every contractor should learn how to develop a referral business. Put door hangers on every door in the neighborhood after the install saying your neighbor just installed a Mitsubishi heat pump (or whatever product was installed). Most neighbors will have similar houses that have similar needs; neighbors talk and will ask about their experiences. Make sure theirs is a positive one; the new sales will be easier to close.

To keep customers as loyal, life-long customers, don't be a stranger. Follow up with every new customer after the first cooling or heating season to ask if their expectations were met and to see if they have any other needs. Ask for referrals without pushing, and thank them again for their business.

In my business, almost 70 percent of my clients comes from referrals. And what better way to get happy customers if not through other happy customers?

Mitsubishi Electric employees should become experts at helping them do this. For more great ideas, there is a great book on referrals called *The Referral Engine* by John Jantsch.

55.
Make Your Marketing About What the Customer Wants

Create your marketing around the positive aspects of your product (i.e., dust-free ductless, energy efficient, and whisper-quiet).

One of the best ways to know what your customers really want is to ask them. Surveying your customers will give you valuable information on the best way to spend your marketing dollars. Do you know what your customers really want? Or are you only selling them what you want to sell them?

> TYPICALLY, WHAT YOUR CUSTOMER WANTS PERTAINS TO SOME TYPE OF LIFESTYLE ISSUE. SELL TO THAT.

Typically, what your customer wants pertains to some type of lifestyle issue. Sell to that. This is one of the key messages used by Mitsubishi Electric, U.S. Cooling & Heating. Here is an example of selling to the lifestyle vs. selling the "product":

What you get is comfort without compromise. Beyond simply regulating the temperature within your space, individual room controls allow you to improve the efficiency of your entire home.

Whether renovating your home or building a new one, in a hot or cold climate, you can end the struggle of cost vs. comfort: use only the exact amount of energy needed to maintain comfort. With a wide range of ENERGY STAR® qualified, whisper-quiet indoor systems delivering allergen filtration that actually cleans the air, Mitsubishi Electric, U.S. Cooling & Heating, systems are the right choice for your home comfort needs.

While people want to make sure they are getting a great product, they typically care more about how it solves their lifestyle need than they do about the product itself.

Once you know what their true want or need is, and you have shared the benefits of your offering, then you can go into explaining how it works and the product features.

Listen and respond to what your customer wants. Below are examples of marketing to what the customer wants.

56.
Understand If You Can't Close, You'll Have Skinny Kids

If you have made the investment to serve your homeowner, there will come a time when there is an expectation that you will ask for a commitment and close the deal.

Zig Ziglar once wrote that if you couldn't close, you are going to have skinny kids. I would add to that if you can't close, you are just an unpaid consultant.

Closing does not have to include conflict, stress, or beating your homeowner into submission. If you have extended yourself emotionally and professionally to your homeowner and laid all the appropriate groundwork in the early stages of the sales process, closing will be a natural part of the conversation. That does not mean the answer will always be yes; it just means there will come a point when it seems natural to bring the conversation to a conclusion—one way or the other. And remember, yes is best but no is a perfectly acceptable answer.

In the old days of selling, it was about the "ABC's"—Always Be Closing. The basic strategy was to spend 10 percent of your time acting like you were interested in your homeowner, and then 90 percent of your time closing, closing, and closing.

You should do just the opposite, investing 90 percent of your time and energy into serving your homeowner. You'll find yourself spending only 10 percent of your time and energy closing.

This does not mean you can ask for the order one time and give up.

Remember, human nature dictates that when given the choice of spending money today or spending it next Tuesday, we will choose next Tuesday. It is critical to know that even if your homeowner likes you, even if your homeowner loves your company, even if your homeowner wants and needs your product and service, even if your homeowner thinks the price is fair and that your offer has tremendous value, he would still prefer to postpone spending his money. It's in our DNA.

So even though closing is less conflicted if you have done your job up front, you will still need to ask for the order several times.

Most of us have learned everything we need to know about closing from our children. When children want something from you it can be a lesson in persistence and closing to behold. It's a thing of beauty when you can step back and analyze it without getting frustrated with your child. They are relentless. They are focused. And they are often successful.

So it goes with your homeowner. They can love you and your company, want and need your product and service, have the money to afford it, and believe it's a great value; yet they will have a tendency to say "no" just because it's their money and they will spend it how and when they please.

So, you may have to ask a few times before your homeowner says "yes." If you ask several times and they say "no," that's okay too. But if you don't ask, you will have to answer to your skinny kids.

Contributed by Weldon Long, who is author of the New York Times *bestseller* The Power of Consistency *and the creator of The HVAC Sales Academy. For more information visit www.HVACSalesAcademy.com.*

57.
Realize It's Not About You

*To gain trust with your buyers, they need to like you
and believe you are there because they have a need that
you can solve; focus on them, not you.*

While building a relationship with your homeowner is fundamental to the selling process, I am not going to insult your intelligence by acting like you've never thought about it before. You are probably pretty good at it, as it's typically the first thing we learn to do in Sales 101.

Although the phrase "people buy from those they like and trust" is a cliché, it is a cliché because it is true. The relationship-building process is your first opportunity to lay the foundation for sales success and to prepare yourself for the end game of earning your homeowner's business.

KEEP THE SPOTLIGHT ON THEM WITH QUESTIONS ABOUT THEM.

Building a relationship with your homeowner always begins with getting them to like you and identifying commonalities when possible. The best way to accomplish both of these is with questions, questions, and questions.

There is no better way to get people to like you than to show genuine interest in them, and there is no better way to show genuine interest in them than asking questions. While it is axiomatic that you can talk about things you share in common like fishing, motorcycles or golf—it is critical to keep it about their fishing, motorcycles or golf, not yours.

When opening the conversation with your homeowner, imagine the two of you are in a dark room and there is a spotlight that shines on whomever is doing the talking - but there is only ONE spotlight, and it can't be on both of you at the same time. Your responsibility is to keep the spotlight on the homeowner. Anytime you feel the heat and the glare of the spotlight on you, you have to get it back on your homeowner. The most effective way to do that is by asking him or her a question.

It is also very helpful to discuss things you have in common with your homeowner.

Many times, in an attempt to draw commonalities with our homeowner, we talk about our fishing, motorcycles, or golf. We want to let them know we like the same things they like. Unfortunately, if you respond to your homeowner's golf stories with your own, it often sounds like you are trying to "one-up" them. Of course, that's not your intent; but all that matters is how it comes across to your homeowner.

Over the course of any sales opportunity, once you've established some commonalities, talk about them. But make sure you talk about the customer's experiences, not your own. You have to keep the spotlight on your homeowner and his or her interests.

Building a relationship with your homeowner is always your first step to sales success, and discussing things you have in common is a great way to start the relationship, just as long as you always keep the questions and stories focused on your prospect.

Contributed by Weldon Long, who is author of the New York Times *bestseller* The Power of Consistency *and the creator of* The HVAC Sales Academy. *For more information visit www.HVACSalesAcademy.com.*

58.
Understand the Other Side of "I Don't Know"

The space between "yes" and "no" is Sales Purgatory. Staying with the sales process until you get a definitive answer will dramatically contribute to your long-term success.

Taking "no" for an answer will not ruin your sales career. In fact, it won't even hurt your career. To the contrary, if you are willing to stay with the sales process until you get a definitive "yes" or "no" from your prospect, you will find yourself among the top performers in sales.

Taking "I don't know" for an answer will undermine your earning potential and destroy your sales performance. This is where all too many sales professionals end the sales process—somewhere between "yes" and "no."

Sales professionals would always prefer to hear the sweetest word in sales, but not everyone is going to say "yes." You will never have a 100% close ratio. You wouldn't even want that; if everyone said "yes" to you, it would mean you would be selling your HVAC systems on the cheap.

The problem is that many sales professionals will directly ask for the order one time, hoping for a "yes." But if they get "I don't know," they will stop, afraid that if they ask again the prospect will give them a definitive "no." Instead, you should beg for a definitive "no."

The key is staying with the process. If you fold after the first "I don't know," you'll never see what's beyond that; and you will never know the feeling of being a top sales performer. You'll never see what's on the other side of "I don't know."

Once you find the courage and confidence to see what's beyond "I don't know," you will be amazed how often your prospect ends up saying "yes."

It's critical to understand human nature and how that plays into your homeowner's initial reaction when you first ask for the order. The first time you ask, your prospect's initial reaction is likely to be "I don't know," because they are evaluating how long they can postpone the purchase or they are stalling to see if you'll drop the price. This is especially true if there is no particular emotional connection between the prospect and your offer. Nevertheless, if you have professionally fulfilled your duties and are willing to stay with the process beyond "I don't know," your homeowner will be inclined to lean toward a yes. It's just human nature to put off a decision if possible.

Be brave. Be courageous. Find out what is on the other side of "I don't know." You will be amazed with the results.

Contributed by Weldon Long, who is author of the New York Times *bestseller* The Power of Consistency *and the creator of The HVAC Sales Academy. For more information visit www.HVACSalesAcademy.com.*

59.
Get to Know Your Local Electric Utility Contact

Staying in the know on the rebates, incentives, and priorities offered by your local utility providers can give you advantages for many of your offerings—hence, more sales.

Get to know who your local electric utility contact is, and reach out to him or her. This is a good idea for a contractor, since there may be resources available that will help you sell more. The utility contact may even be looking for help developing new programs (i.e., designing new ductless/VRF incentive programs).

Your experience is a wealth of knowledge to electric utility staff, and they will appreciate you contacting them and your desire to partner with them. They will also make you aware of any offerings or rebate programs available if specific standards are met. This can be used as additional incentive for your sales team and to validate value to your prospective customers. Your customers will be pleasantly surprised that you have a relationship with the utility company and that you truly care about providing cost-saving, energy efficient solutions for them.

Finally, when the utility company gets leads—which they receive all the time—they will be more likely to send them to you if you have pro-actively sought them out in a partnership fashion to create a mutually beneficial relationship.

Utilize www.dsire.org to identify additional electric rebate opportunities.

60.
Partner with a Trusted Supplier

*Use a trusted supplier's expertise to differentiate
your business, and vice versa. Value their contribution to
your success and reward them with your loyalty.*

There's an old saying: "You will be known by the company you keep." If I asked you who your trusted suppliers were, at least a few people would likely come to mind, each for different reasons and value. If you aren't leveraging your relationships with your trusted suppliers and their expertise, you're missing out on some significant opportunities.

One of the easiest ways to leverage your trusted supplier's expertise is as an extension of your brand. Nothing lends credibility to your own brand like connecting with other credible brands. When you partner with well-respected brands, and you represent yourself as partnering together, you can gain instant trust with potential customers. It will differentiate you from others who are either not leveraging their relationships or who just don't have them.

> **YOU WILL BE KNOWN BY THE COMPANY YOU KEEP.**

Talk with your suppliers and find conscious ways to leverage your relationship for mutual wins, and provide referrals for them where appropriate. Get creative and do things like cross-marketing to share costs and maximize dual exposure.

Take your relationship to the next level, and you will find increased opportunities between you, which means additional revenues.

61.
Handle Objections

*Thinking ahead for potential objections and coming up
with solutions to various objectives will add credibility to you
and the company and remove reasons to say "no."*

The best way to handle objections is to solve them beforehand. Carefully step through your sales presentation and change or get rid of any statements that might create a "no" answer from your prospect.

However, even after "no-proofing" your presentation, it is still very likely that your prospect will have an objection or two that you didn't anticipate. Here are some ideas to help you.

- **Try to mention a point of agreement before you directly answer the objection.** As an example: "Before I get into that, is it fair to say that we all believe something needs to be done about this situation?" This way you build a bridge between you and your audience, and create some distance from the point of contention.
- **Don't be afraid to admit when you are wrong.** Being courageous enough to admit an error can actually help your case. Just don't overdo it. A simple and diplomatic acknowledgment of the mistake is all that's required.
- **Try to defuse the objection.** Find a way to change the words to be positive (or at least neutral) rather than negative. For example, "That costs too much" can be answered with "Let's talk about the value of my product/service to your company." Or, if someone asks, "Why are your prices so high?" you could repeat the question by rephrasing it, "What is the value of our service?"
- **Ask for assistance from team members when you're stumped.** Just say something like, "I'm not sure how to best respond to that concern. Could anyone help me out with that one?"

Develop a list of objections and how to overcome them; then make sure everyone on your team has a copy of this list, understands it, and familiarizes themselves with it, so that when they are faced with an objection, they can speak to it authoritatively in a way that is credible.

62.
Make Financing Available on Every Proposal

Financing is a critical tool to increasing closure rates and upselling a customer (owner). Ensure you have options.

Making a purchasing decision for heating and cooling can be a costly one for a homeowner. With other priorities competing for cash, there is a growing trend among contractors to offer financing options. While there are some pros and cons, the key is to make the payment affordable and provide some clarity.

Offering finance options can significantly reduce your sales cycle and get the close. Due to cost, customers will often put off making a buying decision that isn't absolutely necessary if it means making a large cash outlay up front. Financing also affords an opportunity to promote the Preferred Customer Agreement and other upsell offerings that can be bundled together into one financing option, thus increasing your transaction size and profit margins.

Today, buyers want options. And the more flexible you are and the greater the offering, the more you will be seen as a valued service provider.

Start with the 60-month affordable payment option only (with reduced rate interest). Used by itself, it is the only way that the addition of financing on every proposal is going to be capturing additional business. Offering low monthly payments despite the interest is a way to create a "feel good" option for everyone that can use the help of a loan.

As an added bonus to the buyer, consider offering a no-interest clause for a short-term finance. That will ensure you get your money back quickly and will create consistent cash flow.

LEADERSHIP

63.
Live by Documented "Personal Standards"

Develop a set of standards—10 is a good number—of the most important things for creating success and what you want to be known for. Then live them daily.

IF YOU HAVE A PERSONAL STANDARD CENTERED AROUND ACCELERATING YOUR RESULTS, YOU'LL PERFORM TASKS WITH ACCELERATED TIME FRAMES ASSOCIATED WITH THEM.

If you've ever worked for or been exposed to a large company, you probably know what corporate standards are, and how a standard transmits to the culture. Cultures are built on the standards of the organization, and some business owners and contractors go to great lengths to create cultures that reflect their personal standards.

We both have specific personal defined standards. These are more than just beliefs; they're values and standards that we live by. I (Tony) have twelve specific standards and I know them well, but I also have them written down. They include meeting my teams' inspirational needs each day; looking at my client pipeline; studying my daily to-do list; eating, exercising, and living healthy; and doing favors in advance for people. Peter's include having gratitude each day, telling his wife and friends "I love you," exercising, and making healthy choices.

Be aware of what standards you want to incorporate into your daily life. Think of what they are, write them down, and reassess them. Standards on speed, for instance, are generally very low. Today we have technology that equips us to do more, and in a quicker time frame. You no longer have to wait until Monday at the office to review a document, for instance. If you have a personal standard centered around accelerating your results, you'll perform tasks with accelerated time frames associated with them.

The person with the highest standards is the person who lives in mastery. If you don't want to have high standards, be average. Some people are okay with average, mediocre results. But you're probably reading this because you want more than that, so develop personal standards that you and everyone around you can live by.

Tony's Personal Daily Standards

Like your business standards, your Personal Daily Standards are those standards which you strive to live by and operate from. This can include a spiritual side, some of your prior business standards, and any other items that are important to you that help you run a happy and healthy life.

1. Ask in **Prayer** for smartness and Holy Spirit support and alignment with God's will

2. Do team **huddles** and stimulate huddles

3. Glance at "**pipe**" each am to have actions fresh in mind

4. Determine **VIPs** for the day – (from Master list)

5. Touch Team members **inspirationally**.

6. Communicate **appreciation** to all those around me (personal and professional)

7. Strength, flex and **breathe** with confidence and think gratitude

8. **Organize** (rationalize) so more good things can come in

9. **Visualize** with further "clarity" our goals, direction, vision and refinement

10. **Model** exceptional behavior including enjoying life

11. Eat **healthy**

12. Do **favors** and help advance my clients' success

64.
Make Your Goals Known

Ensure your employees know your company goals; talk about them, brainstorm them, and post them on the walls where possible. To get what you want, you have to know what you want.

Peter and I are both into goals so much that combined we have over 200 pages of goals and accomplishments. Why such a dedication to goals?

Goals help to focus energy, form plans, live a purpose-centered life, and give a feeling of accomplishment. A goal is an observable and measurable end result that you intend to achieve or accomplish. A well-planned goal also includes some sort of timeframe.

Clear and compelling goals form the foundations for your success. Simply put, we need to find out where we are going—and know who we are—before we set out on the journey.

When you as the leader set clear and inspiring goals for the company, you and your team will almost be *pulled toward* your desired outcome.

Forcing motivation can become a thing of the past. When everyone is moving toward a common goal where everyone benefits, there is inspiration and motivation.

Post your written company goals somewhere every employee can see daily. Talk about them in company meetings, and share successes that have to do with achieving specific goals. Measure yourself and the overall company performance against those goals regularly.

65.
Lead the Way

*One of the most important ways to get others to live
out your goals and vision is to lead the way. Be someone
the team respects and wants to model.*

Leadership is extremely important. Your business can't survive without your leadership, but what is a leader? Are leaders born? Are they made? No, leadership is earned.

You can't force people to follow you and your vision; you have to lead the way. Does every person in your company know your vision? If not, what are you doing to lead them in the direction you want the company to go? Are you clear on the direction you want to take your company? Is service the focus of your company? Then having a mission statement that puts service on a pedestal is of the utmost importance.

Reward good service and good follow up. Treat your employees as if they are your most valued asset...because they are! If employees don't feel they are important to you, not only will they not follow you as the leader, they will not have the company's best interest at heart on every call.

Here is an example of good leadership:

A company was experiencing a significant number of callbacks. It seemed like every time they did a new installation, they ended up going back. This happened on many of the service calls, as well. The company was losing a great deal of money on these callbacks. It is very hard to charge the customer for something you didn't do right the first time.

So this company had a contest. They put the number of callbacks each technician had for the previous month up on a white board in the shop for everyone to see. Of course the really experienced technicians had less; the newer, less seasoned techs had more. What do you supposed happened immediately? The older technicians gave the "green" guys a hard time, but then took them under their wing and helped them get better. The herd policed itself; and to top it all off, the employer gave a $100 bonus each month to the tech that had the lowest number of callbacks. Do you think you could motivate employees to dot all their "I's" and cross all their "T's" for an extra bonus and better social standing among their peers? I think so, and it worked for this company.

It all comes back to leadership. That boss had the direction, fewer callbacks, and better service, and now the employees see that he means it. He set them on the path to becoming better technicians, and allowed the more experienced guys to spend time training the younger technicians.

66.
Survey Your Company Culture

To gain valuable information, ask your people to fill out an internal survey that has perhaps 7–10 questions of how your business can perform better. Do this twice a year.

A business with a great strategy but bad culture can still fail.

Are you a leader who promotes out-of-the-box thinking, or do the words "that will never happen around here" echo through your halls?

A company's culture is similar to an individual's personality. It is made up of the collective values, terminology, customs, beliefs, habits, and attitudes shared by each of the team members. Company culture influences everything from how customers perceive us to employee morale to the sense of urgency with which things get done.

It is important to *know*—and not just *assume* you know—the true culture that has developed inside your company. Equally important is to know the general mood of your people. How do they perceive the company—the good, the bad, and the ugly? What do they see that perhaps you do not?

In order for your people to feel confident enough to answer honestly, they have to trust you and know you'll take action, even if the results aren't exactly where you wanted them to be.

A sample survey is available to download free in Mitsubishi Contractor Toolkit, at www.mitsubishipro.com/toolkit.

Sample Survey for Company Culture	
1. What do you want to be doing in five years?	
2. How do you propose to get there?	
3. What can you do for this company to improve it tomorrow?	
4. What is your goal for income for the next two years?	
5. Would you eventually like my job?	
6. How can we better help you do what you're doing?	
7. What technology could we be utilizing that we aren't currently?	

67.
Build Systems for Everything

"Systems pay off short term and long term.
They support efficiency, consistency, and follow through,
which becomes a part of your culture."

A system is simply a set of processes that can be operated independently of you, such as including how a new person starts with your company, how you reset tools, and more. The more your business grows and the more you're responsible for, the more important these systems become.

To consistently produce the right results, we must ensure that the same *process* is utilized—over and over again. Systems are the rules, policies, and procedures put in place that trained staff can replicate without relying on your involvement.

It is important to build systems for as many organizational actions as possible. Put these into your employee handbook, train your new hires, and ensure an ongoing commitment to utilizing these systems.

Here are some suggestions on installation and sales procedures:

Sales & Installation Procedures

Installation
1. Check parts and make sure everything is present to complete the job (before going).
2. Understand the time sequence for the job.
3. Ask the customer exactly what they want and what their expectations are (potentially utilizing a survey sheet); make sure nothing has changed since last contact. Number-one priority is a satisfied customer.
4. Be aware of time and stick to the schedule while always doing a good job.
5. Conduct a walk-through with customer to confirm expectations are met

Sales
1.   Phone: set up appointment (utilize script/outline for call).
2.   First face-to-face
a.   Be clear on product knowledge and what the costumer can expect.
b.   Have prepared list of common objections and answers.
c.   Clearly explain options and have solutions to the overall problem the customer is trying to solve.
d.   Be prepared to give a price.
e.   Have a contract ready to sign (include the timing sequence of project in the contract).
3.   After Installation
a.   Either phone or in person, follow-up to ensure satisfaction.
b.   Soft sell referrals for new leads (potentially utilize small incentive).

68.
Handle Setbacks

Setbacks are inevitable in life, no matter how many things you do right. How you deal with them can make or break your future.

> DISAPPOINTMENTS, FAILURES, AND SETBACKS ARE A NORMAL PART OF THE LIFECYCLE OF A COMPANY. WHAT THE LEADER HAS TO DO IS CONSTANTLY BE UP AND SAY, "WE HAVE A PROBLEM; LET'S GO AND GET IT."
>
> – COLIN POWELL

One of the things I (Tony) do with my team after every session or event is a process called "Correction of Errors" or COEs. Because nothing is perfect, we are continually searching for better ways and asking ourselves "What could we have done better or differently?" Doing this without becoming defeated when things don't go as planned will continue to make you more solid.

Oftentimes, it is those exact setbacks that become great opportunities to take a new and more promising approach to any problem, and come back even stronger the next time.

For us, our COEs on a session might look something like this:
- Fix typo on slide 8
- Exercise on High-Leverage Activities was rushed
- Test speaker volume prior to session
- Add examples when sharing about creating an arsenal

69.
Give Praise and Show Gratitude

People want to be recognized, appreciated, and feel like they are important to you and the company.

Few things inspire and motivate people more than to feel like they have value to you and that their work is appreciated and noticed. Roll up your sleeves and help your team...a great leader should be dynamically involved.

Your gratitude and encouragement can be shown in small ways, too, like through texts, email, notes, and gift cards. Show the world how much you appreciate your people.

- A great executive inspires—rather than crushes—his team.
- Recognize the little things, not just the big things.
- Challenge your team to catch someone doing something *right*.

Facilitate a simple compliment activity whereby people use index cards during a meeting. Each person has an index card with his or her name as a title. By rotation, the cards are passed to all other team members, who write a complimentary phrase on each person's card, and the rotation is continued until the cards go back to the original owner. Then each card owner reads and shares the top one or two phrases on his or her card.

This is a great way to show leadership and appreciation, as well as to encourage teambuilding, all in one exercise.

70.
Acknowledge Different Perspectives

Instead of insisting on always BEING right, focus on the right outcome. Be open to new ideas and other people's way of doing things.

When someone makes a great suggestion that differs somewhat from our own ideas—whether it's in a public meeting or one-on-one—we can have a much greater impact by letting that person be right than by contradicting them. If we're really honest with ourselves, we'll see that often it's not that the person's idea is wrong—it's just not the same as ours.

Sometimes our ego gets in the way of letting other people be right— especially if we think we can "one-up" them! As tempted as we may be to promote our own idea, method, or strategy over another person's, it's often far more impactful to let that person win and be right. (I wonder how many marriages could be saved if both partners practiced this distinction!)

Look for ways to help people win. Make them smile or laugh, and help them enjoy life. Ask about their goals and see how you can help them. My friend Zig Ziglar said, "You will get everything in life that you want if you just help enough other people get what they want." It's true! When you create win-win opportunities at home, in the workplace, or in your presentations, you allow most everyone to benefit and succeed.

PEOPLE

71.
Appreciate
(and Invest Time in)
What You Want More of
(Good People)

*When you're focused and verbally appreciate something specific,
people want to do more of it. It's that simple.*

If you want to grow your portfolio, you'll have to invest. This basic
rule applies to all areas in life.

Appreciate what you want more of in other areas of your life, not just
finances. Invest in the lives of loved
ones to solidify your relationships.
There are six basic elements common to all human existence, and
how we combine them provides the
evidence of our life management.
This concept is also known by many
as the "Balance Wheel of Life," and
it embraces the principle that the
more balanced we are in each of the
six areas, the smoother our wheel
of life will roll. We say it's not really
about focusing on perfect balance;
it's about managed balance. For ex-

ample, when you're in your early twenties, you often want to be out of
balance and be heavy on education; or if you have someone in your
family who needs extra care because of health, you want to invest extra
time supporting them.

When you verbally appreciate something specific, people want to do more of it. It's that simple.

This concept moves all the way down to even what you say or write on any given day. I (Tony) send texts to my girls almost daily, appreciating them for making good decisions; and they have become incredible young adults who make exceptional decisions. And I continue to appreciate this with the focused thinking of wanting more and more positive daily decisions from my kids.

> KNOW WHAT REALLY, REALLY MAKES YOU HAPPY, THEN BUILD A LIFE AROUND IT.
>
> –TONY JEARY

Our families are one of God's greatest gifts. We are charged with the responsibility of nurturing family relationships, with the overall goal of creating happy, secure, and successful families. The common threads of faithfulness and commitment hold successful families together, for those attributes create an atmosphere of love and trust in which families can thrive. If you want a great family, invest in them and appreciate them—a lot! Likewise, if you want a healthy company or a healthy body, invest in it and the results will multiply.

72.
Help Others Win, Especially Your Team

"True success begins with happy and fulfilled employees, vendors, suppliers, and family. Identify what inspires and motivates your team; then help them accomplish."

From day one, we encounter competition—on the playground, in the classroom, on the playing field. Later we compete with others for grades, educational benefits, careers, and achievements. It seems we are wired to compete (at some level), and that often leads to a mindset of "one-upping," outshining, and outperforming others. But truly smart high achievers help others win, which directly impacts the speed of results they experience. This is a principle both Peter and Tony live out today.

When Tony was a kid, his dad taught him the most important business principle of his life: "Give value: Do more than is expected!" It is the foundation of his success, and in fact, his entire business centers around helping their clients win often by giving value and doing more than what is expected.

Peter also loves to over-deliver and add value to another's life and growth. And when we first decided to write this book, we knew we both shared this philosophy. It is the foundation of the success we both enjoy.

Bottom line: Successful people help others become successful too. This rule is powerful because it requires a paradigm shift for many. Those who cannot make the paradigm shift from a "scarcity, win at all costs" mentality to a "winning by helping others win" mindset will not operate in mastery. In order to be the best, have the best, and deliver the

> SUCCESSFUL PEOPLE HELP OTHERS BECOME SUCCESSFUL TOO

best results, you must be completely comfortable and confident that you will win when you help others win—it's a must.

How many times have you encountered a colleague or service provider who seemed to enjoy saying no? They want to give as little as possible, and they feel good doing it. Sooner or later, that person's business will suffer.

We've all heard the term "buyer's remorse." It is a polite term for the way people feel when they have purchased something or decided on something and the item or the experience perhaps did not meet their felt needs and expectations. The negatives of disappointment are significant, but there is a huge positive impact on results when products or services exceed expectations.

When we buy something that exceeds our expectations, we are often blown away by our good fortune. We can't believe that we "got all of this" for what we paid. What we got could be a combination of product, quality, customer support, the effect the product had on our lives, or any other thing that makes us happy about the money we spent. When our expectations are exceeded, we become walking advertisements and testimonials for the product or service. Every time we run across a friend with a similar need, we tell them about what we got for what we paid. We are what Ken Blanchard calls "raving fans" at that point, and a raving fan can't be tempted and lured away by competitors. This is the kind of customer that leads to growth and great results for any business.

When you help someone win, you often create a fan for life. Embed this rule into your organization. Often when I'm making a presentation, I'll facilitate input. If someone says something that is very valuable, I have two choices. I can "gloss over it" by saying something like "that's a good idea," and then continue spouting my great ideas (which many people do). Or I can have a much greater impact with my audience—and especially with that individual—if I compliment the person on the great idea and encourage him or her to share more. I might say something like, "Wow! That's really a great idea, Bob! Tell us more!" By doing so, I create a triple win: Bob wins (I let him shine), the other audience members win (they have received valuable input from someone other than me), and I win (I gained trust, respect, and rapport by letting someone else shine).

Think about all the people in your life—customers, vendors, suppliers, family, and employees. Figure out what they want and help them constantly move toward that.

73.
Surround Yourself With Successful, Positive People

Search for, find, and be around successful people who have the right attitude, inspire, and motivate; eliminate those who don't.

We all have a choice about whom we spend time with. And with all the billions of people on this planet, life is simply too short not to spend your valuable time with inspiring ones. Gravitate toward the people who make you happy and who support and motivate you; and gravitate away from people who are negative, uninspiring, angry, or self-defeating. And that, of course, includes whom you hire. Are you surrounded by dream-killers? Or are you surrounded by positive and inspiring people?

FIND SUCCESSFUL PEOPLE WHO INSPIRE AND MOTIVATE YOU TO ACHIEVE YOUR GOALS, NO MATTER HOW BIG YOUR VISION IS.

You can tell a lot about an individual by the things that make them angry, the things they focus on, and the ways they spend their time. Are they bitter, upset, or thinking of ways to beat down a competitor? Do they go on and on about small, meaningless, negative conflict and focus on the bad things that happen to them? Successful people do not think that way.

Eliminate the toxic people and naysayers who drag you down or make you feel bad. If you can't eliminate them, at least reduce the time you spend with those people. Don't surround yourself with negative people who are not motivating you each day. Find successful people who inspire and motivate you to achieve your goals, no matter how big your vision is.

Find action-oriented people who have done what you want to do. These people are the momentum who will hold you accountable, yet also inspire you to achieve your true potential.

Hire people who have different strengths than you. If you are weak in an area, hire someone who is strong in that area. Do not hire people that are a mirror of yourself.

IT'S NOT ABOUT THE GRADES YOU MAKE AS MUCH AS IT IS ABOUT THE HANDS YOU SHAKE— CHERISH AND BUILD RELATIONSHIPS.

–TONY JEARY

74.
Maintain Harmony on the Home Front

Balance your resources, energy,
and time to create the business and life you want.

Balance your energy and your time. That statement is easier said than done. In today's fast-paced world, one of the most difficult things to achieve at times is balance. And while it may not be possible to get the exact balance you want each and every day, you can prioritize your resources, energy and time to get more of what you and your family want.

> **MAKE YOUR BUSINESS GOALS CONGRUENT WITH MAINTAINING YOUR FAMILY GOALS, AND KEEP YOUR FAMILY A PRIORITY.**

Living the life of a business owner can sometimes create financial and emotional stress. If you aren't careful, this can often spill over into your home life, affecting our spouse, children, and relationships. If your spouse and family aren't happy, oftentimes the business won't be taken care of either. Since nothing is done in a vacuum, it is important to take a holistic approach to success—not just in business, but also in life.

Spend some time documenting your goals as a family. Make the effort to include your spouse in the big picture decisions and make sure he or she is on board. And then make sure your business practices are in alignment with your family values and goals.

Below are some activities that can help identify and maintain total life congruence. For additional tools, email info@tonyjeary.com for an electronic copy of *Designing Your Own Life*.

Family Priorities

It is important to communicate together and discuss who you want to be as a family. It promotes unity with your spouse and children and gives standards to operate by together. Having a family mission statement helps ensure that your family operates intentionally and not accidentally.

Family Mission Statement & Commitment

Together with your family, write your mission statement below as well as things you commit to doing together and qualities to espouse. For your mission statement, keep it to 12-15 words when possible.

We commit to doing together these 5 things as much as possible:	We will show everyone, including ourselves, these 5 qualities all the time:
1.	1.
2.	2.
3.	3.
4.	4.
5.	5.

10 Things that are Important to MY SPOUSE

1.

2.

3.

4.

5.

6.

7.

8.

9.

10.

Things to Commit to Together for Our Relationship

1.

2.

3.

4.

5.

75.
Assemble and Manage Superstar Employee Relationships

"Hire people with savvy, current skills, and winning personalities. Carefully putting the right team members together based on personality styles, skills, and relationships will create the best synergies and results."

Now more than ever, it pays to be sensitive to the needs of the employee. The old philosophy of an 8 to 5 office job is becoming increasingly obsolete. Having a flexible work schedule as well as flexibility in roles and responsibilities is quickly becoming the new normal. If you want to keep superstar employees, you have to compensate them and show them a clear path of upward mobility.

So much of what I (Tony) do and teach has to do with teamwork—people helping people. None of us—me included—would be successful without the help of others. Thankfully, God has blessed each one of us with unique qualities; and because we're all different, we can fill in the gaps for each other. Where one is weak, another is strong.

FOR MORE ABOUT GETTING THE RIGHT PEOPLE ON YOUR TEAM, READ THE BOOK *GOOD TO GREAT* BY JIM COLLINS.

Everyone on my core team has both different and overlapping talents—that's why I handpicked each one of them. I appreciate their ability to execute with their special gifts to complete the puzzle when we are servicing our clients. We all work together to make a whole, and I make sure they know how valuable they are to me by constantly finding ways to show my appreciation.

Michael Cappuccio provides three great points regarding "Great Employees":

- Happy employees produce results. Results produce profits.
- Don't just fill holes with new hires; look for *great* new hires.
- Respect them and respect will be returned. It will create a productive, happy environment and will result in more profits.

Here are some ideas to remember when hiring:

1. When running an ad, remember that you're selling an opportunity, not just offering a job, and write the ad accordingly.
2. Establish a reward system to encourage your employees to refer qualified candidates.
3. Always prepare a job description, which we now call performance expectations, before you post a job ad.

76.
Keep Your People Motivated

"Keeping people motivated creates loyalty and reduces turnover. Recognize them, appreciate them, provide competitive wages, and make them know you genuinely care about them."

Research has shown that, typically, employees are motivated by the following things:

1. Recognition or appreciation
2. Interesting work
3. Wages
4. Awareness of what's going on in the company
5. Good working conditions
6. Job security
7. Feeling that management cares about the employee

Entrepreneurs are generally motivated by one or more of the following:

1. Creativity or growth
2. Money
3. Power
4. Freedom
5. Survival

Although there is some overlap, the real takeaway here is that what motivates you as an employer is often very different from what motivates your employees. Knowing how your employees think is of utmost importance.

One of the ways to make sure your employees feel heard and connected is to incorporate an "Active Suggestion System," as utilized by Richard Harshaw. He has found that using this system keeps morale high and employees invested. It gives employees a sense of ownership and presents the company with options to expand opportunities and/or trim costs. At its essence, the system looks like this:

- Set up a suggestion box
- Suggestions are reviewed by an employee committee (voted on by peers)
- Committee accepts or rejects with management approval
- Set up an employee meeting to announce the idea; give the team a week to nominate and elect representatives to a review committee. The committee will meet monthly.
- Use the ARM approach. The committee reviews each suggestion and discusses. After the discussion, the suggestion is assigned a letter:
  - A = Accepted
  - R = Rejected
  - M = see Management to explore further
  - For ideas that save money (that can be documented), the employee who submitted the suggestion is given a percentage of the annual savings in a year-end bonus.

77.
Develop an "On-Boarding" Process for New Employees

The right "on-boarding" process will ensure all new employees understand your standards, values, and goals and will create consistent habits of execution in the field. It is one of the best ways to ensure your brand is being represented as you want it to be.

GOOD ON-BOARDING COSTS ONLY A FRACTION OF THE COST OF HIGH TURNOVER.

One of the biggest expenses a contractor can have is employee turnover. In fact, statistics show that as high as 46 percent of new hires don't last 18 months. It is expensive to hire and train new people and costs a significant amount of valuable time as well. Good on-boarding costs only a fraction of the cost of high turnover.

To access some good on-boarding programs for the contracting industry, go to www.Dsire.org. They have a variety of links to on-boarding software, videos, programs, etc. Choose the type of program you want, and all the information is there in one place for you to choose from.

A successful on-boarding process and program can ensure the smooth transition of new employees into your company culture. You can also create an operations manual to drive consistency throughout the organization.

78.
Incentivize Your Employees to Educate Themselves

*Contractor employees tend to maintain the status quo
and not learn and change the way they conduct business.
By learning, they not only improve themselves, but also their
employer (you), and ultimately, the customer.*

Think about it, what greater incentive program can there be than getting employees to want to educate themselves? It's a total win-win for you and for them. It also says to your employees that they matter and that you are committed to making the company and the workplace a great place to be.

Contractors can create incentives in a number of ways: offer tuition reimbursement for successfully completing and passing a training, offer financial rewards in the way of bonus or pay increases for self-development, or even offer a promotion for certain levels of achievement and education.

> **WHAT GREATER INCENTIVE PROGRAM CAN THERE BE THAN GETTING EMPLOYEES TO WANT TO EDUCATE THEMSELVES? IT'S A TOTAL WIN-WIN FOR YOU AND FOR THEM.**

NATE offers many certification programs as well as CEUs, and there may be additional opportunities for appropriate training at local or online universities.

An investment in your employees is an investment in your company that will pay off for you both in the long run. It not only builds a more educated work force, but also adds credibility and expertise to the organization.

79.
Take Advantage of and Conduct Training

Understanding the product increases familiarity and confidence, and your entire organization will win.

Product training needs to be embedded into your company culture. The more your employees know, the better they will be at maximizing sales opportunities and creating loyal, satisfied customers. Training also helps minimize mistakes and thus saves profit dollars.

THERE ARE OFTEN CLASSES OFFERED BY MANUFACTURERS AND DISTRIBUTORS. TAKING ADVANTAGE OF THEM WILL CREATE MORE EXPERTISE WITHIN.

Companies oftentimes believe they have to conduct the training themselves, so they skip this important lesson due to time constraints and lack of material. Instead, leverage TMs to provide training, and take advantage of comprehensive training offered by the manufacturers.

In fact, Mitsubishi Electric, U.S. Cooling & Heating, has comprehensive training that you should be leveraging, if you aren't already. They train more than 10,000 people a year, offering training courses nearly every week at each of their five training centers, with a schedule published a year in advance. Classes include selling, installation, service warranty and repair, and more. One of the most popular courses is "Get in the Zone," which focuses on marketing and growth opportunity for the ductless technology community.

They also have a Training & Development website driven by their Learning Management System. That site offers:

- CEUs for commercial and residential training
- Password-protected accounts for all training customers
- Online registration available for all their training programs
- 24/7 access to your training history

They have training on selling, installation, service, warranty, and repair. You need to be participating in and leveraging this incredible wealth of knowledge.

One unique way to leverage training is to invite manufacturers or company personnel to present on a specific product monthly or quarterly. This would allow for training of new personnel, as well as bringing project managers up to date with products they may already be familiar with.

You can also leverage industry training through companies like ACCA, NexStar Network®, and Dsire.org. These organizations offer a full schedule of contractor training.

Investing in your employees and being dedicated to continuous improvement programs for them will create a culture committed to excellence and one people will want to be a part of long-term. It will increase the value of your teams when they are fully equipped to better sell, install, and service your offerings.

80.
Listen More, Talk Less

You don't need to tell your audience everything you know. Tell them only what they need to hear to be persuaded to accept your message.

Boring an audience is a terrible thing. But even worse is the presenter who doesn't know when to quit talking.

Just because you have done your research and uncovered lots of interesting statistics, that doesn't mean you have to share it all. Good presenters don't do a data dump on an audience. They tailor and trim their message to make it meaningful for their particular client/audience in a way that will influence a positive decision. You don't need to tell your audience everything you know. Tell them only what they need to hear to be persuaded to accept your message.

The vast majority of presentations could be done more effectively in less time—often significantly less time. How many presentations have you been a part of that at the end you *really* wished the presenter had spoken longer? The old "less is more" adage is a good one to remember when in front of an audience.

Listening matters. When we ask good questions we are more likely to get responses worth listening to and answers that have valuable information for us personally or professionally. If you want to increase your impact and accomplish even better results, become a master at listening and asking the right questions.

MONEY

81.
Establish a Relationship With a Banker Who Likes You

Every entrepreneur and leader needs a bank—and most importantly a banker who knows and understands you, and enjoys helping you win.

If you're an entrepreneur who has ever tried to secure a loan from a bank, you are well aware of the challenges and frustrations that this process can pose. If you have never had a good banking relationship, it's time to get one.

Some banks are very large and complex entities, and getting any kind of assistance requires jumping through hoops and filling out mountains of paperwork. There's a process to everything, but the bigger the bank, the bigger the process. Traditional banks have traditional goals. If you're an entrepreneur, find a banker with an entrepreneurial mindset.

> **IF YOU HAVE NEVER HAD A GOOD BANKING RELATIONSHIP, IT'S TIME TO GET ONE.**

An entrepreneurial banker will not be so caught up in process flow. He will view your deal with an entrepreneurial mindset, and you will have a greater chance of success if you choose someone who thinks the way you do. Choose the right players to fuel and fund your goals, and begin building essential relationships. This includes the right banker.

Here are some tips taken from *Getting to Yes with your Banker* by Ron Sturgeon and Greg Morse:

How to Choose (and Court) a Banker
Spend some time researching the banks that are accessible to you and finding out which ones would best meet your needs.

Lesson No. 1 – Looking for the Right Banker

- Don't try to fool a banker; they've seen it all and know it when they see *all hat and no cattle.*
- A better way is to find out where someone else banks and get them to refer you.
- You don't want someone who's too young or green, and you don't want someone who's about to retire.

Lesson No. 2 – Creating a Relationship With a Banker

- The business owner has to have confidence that the banker is going to lend him or her money, and the bank has to have confidence that the owner is going to pay it back.

Lesson No. 3 – Expanding Your Banking Relationships

- If you're not dealing with the vice president or above, you are probably dealing with the wrong person.
- You want to meet the people there – the lending officer, the credit officer, and all the other officers you can. And you have to know that you're comfortable with the way they're going to treat you.

Lesson No. 4 – One Size Does Not Fit All

- Generally speaking, the underwriting policies at big banks are not going to give you credit for your experience; they're not going to give you credit for your character. You need to be at a community bank.
- You want to know what your individual lender's loan authority is before you make that decision.
- Every bank has its own procedures, so you'll need to learn those. Ask; they will usually tell you the amounts and the processes.

Lesson No. 5 – Getting What You Want, How You Want It

- A second bank gives customers the option of accessing money that the first bank might not be willing to loan.
- Having a second bank isn't about being able to shave another quarter of a percentage point off a loan rate; it's about being able to get what's best for you and your business.

82.
Pay Average Salaries and Higher Bonuses

"Most successful people surround themselves with like-minded people who are vested in their success almost as much as they are. To keep your great players committed and aligned with you, pay them in a way that incentivizes them when targets are accomplished."

Research your industry and know the average pay. Then be creative with bonuses so people with great results get paid more than virtually anywhere else they can plug into.

If you want to create true "partnerships," pay people in a way that makes them believe their expertise is valued and that they have everything to win by staying engaged with you. If constructed properly, when other team members are winning, you will be winning at an exponential rate. Expect excellence in accordance with the level of compensation. When you do this, all stakeholders win.

EXPECT EXCELLENCE IN ACCORDANCE WITH THE LEVEL OF COMPENSATION.

"Performance Pay for Installers," by Richard Harshaw

- Rather than pay installers an hourly wage (and asking them to work faster) or a flat rate (so many dollars to install a ductless system), tell the crew up front how many hours are built into the job; if they beat the clock, they each get a bonus of half the time they saved on the job.
- On hourly systems, when the job is done in the early afternoon, the crew does not clock off until the end of the day, wasting valuable time. But if they can clock off the job and get a bonus, and then *start*

their next job that afternoon, productivity can soar.

- Have a pre-job meeting to go over the job and share the labor target; when a crew clocks off early, figure the savings of time and give the crew 1/2 of the difference as a bonus check. This can help remove the "stigma" that ductless jobs take too much time.

To increase the productivity ratio, we need a reward system that encourages our installers to do the job in less time so we can do more jobs in a given time. In short, we need to find a way to do more work with the same people. But how?

> STRIP YOUR COMPANY
> OF CASH FROM TIME
> TO TIME SO THAT YOU
> BECOME PERSONALLY
> RICH AS WELL AS
> CORPORATELY RICH.
> –TONY JEARY

Every time you do a job take-off, you must make an estimate for the amount (in hours) and cost (in dollars) of labor. The thing is, most of your installers probably don't make exactly the wage you used for the cost estimate. For instance, you might use a labor cost of $20 per hour for estimating, knowing that only one of your seven installers makes $20 an hour. (Perhaps of the other six, five make less and one makes more.)

Here is how you can provide incentives for your installers to bring jobs in under the time you estimated for them. Before the job is given to the installer (or, if you use two-person crews, the crew), explain that the job was estimated with so many hours of labor. If the job is completed in less time, they will earn a bonus equal to, say, half of the hours by which they beat the estimate.

Remember to put everything in writing and reward for mutually agreed upon goals.

For more information, visit www.salary.com.

83.
Know Your Financial Basics

Know and use your Critical Success Factors to track your success (Profit, Accounts Payable, Accounts Receivable, Cash Flow, Assets, Liabilities, and Net Worth).

Your Critical Success Factors (CSF) are the key areas of your business that determine your effectiveness and, ultimately, your results. Here are a few of the CSFs that are worth not just knowing, but mastering.

- **Profit** – What is left over after subtracting cost of goods and expenses from sales.
- **Accounts payable** – The money owed to your vendors who provide you with goods and services.
- **Accounts receivable** – The money due from your customers that purchase your parts and labor.
- **Cash flow** – Cash flow is the total money coming in and going out through various transactions with clients and vendors.
- **Assets** – Includes all equipment, inventory, real estate, etc.
- **Liabilities** – Outstanding debt to be paid.
- **Net worth** – The amount left over after you subtract your liabilities from your assets.

> CONTINUALLY MEASURING YOUR PROGRESS ALLOWS YOU TO MAKE ADJUSTMENTS AND UNCOVER NEEDED CHANGE.

Continually measuring your progress allows you to make adjustments and uncover needed change, as well as the additional resources you will need to ensure you accomplish what you want to make a reality.

See the Mitsubishi Electric Toolkit at www.mitsubishipro.com/toolkit.

84.
Know Exactly What Your Labor Cost Is for Each of Your Employees

Many contractors don't understand their true costs and underbid jobs. Know your costs so that you can be competitive and make a profit.

It is important to calculate your true labor costs when bidding on projects. For most contractors, labor cost is the single largest expense, which also creates the biggest margin for underbidding jobs if all costs are not considered when giving quotes. If this is done on a consistent basis, it can cripple a business and eliminate profits.

> HOURLY WAGES ARE NOT THE ONLY THING THAT GOES INTO LABOR COSTS.

Hourly wages are not the only thing that goes into labor costs. Other costs include (but are not limited to):

- State and federal payroll taxes (Social Security, FICA, unemployment),
- Vacation, sick days, and other paid time off
- Employee benefits, including insurance (health, disability, life, etc.), bonuses, and retirement plan contributions
- Workers' compensation and liability and auto insurance
- Training expenses
- Job-related clothing, safety gear and tools
- Company-provided vehicles, cell phones, and tablets.

Once you calculate the additional costs associated with carrying an employee, it is equally important to properly calculate the number of hours it should take to complete a specific job. And be sure to include drive time from one job to another—you want to be sure that you aren't eating the expense of necessary unproductive time, but that it is all calculated within the bid so that you can make a profit.

Once you understand and project the true labor costs, you can accurately offer a fair bid to your customer and build a solid financial business with profits.

For additional information on labor costs and to see a spreadsheet, go to the Mitsubishi Contractor Toolkit at www.mitsubishipro.com/toolkit.

85.
Be Clear On the True Cost of Goods

Have costs covered in general; analyze metrics and CSFs. Know the upfront costs of the products, but also the cost of installation and warranty so that you price smartly every time.

SIMPLY PUT, IF YOU HAVE THE EXPENSE ONLY BECAUSE YOU ARE SELLING THE MATERIAL OR SERVICE, IT'S COGS.

The definition of "Cost of Goods Sold" (COGS) is the cost of goods that have been removed from inventory and delivered to the customer.

COGS is any and every cost you incur to buy items for resale, have them delivered to you, store them (if appropriate), and install them. Simply put, if you have the expense only because you are selling the material or service, it's COGS.

Typical examples of COGS are materials purchased for resale; subcontractors or vendors you hire specifically for preparing material for sale; shipping materials like packaging; freight costs of receiving the resale materials; and payroll/labor costs of your employees who are directly related to preparing the goods to be sold or shipped out. (Ask yourself, would you have hired them if you didn't have the materials to sell.)

Costs that are not directly related to getting the materials out the door are considered Operating Expenses and include things like your liability insurance premiums, telephones, office supplies, advertising, clerical payroll, employee benefits, and health insurance for the employees. These expenses would be considered costs of managing the paperwork for the overall business. These are your overhead expenses that you have on an ongoing basis.

86.
Manage Against A Budget

Make stronger decisions by having a well-thought-out budget.

Managing against a budget gives you power and allows you to have better control over you spending decisions. The following are key benefits of having a strong budget:

- **Provides Knowledge.** Budgeting is a valuable tool leading you on a road of financial self-discovery. It allows you to learn exactly how much money is coming in, how fast it goes out, and where it goes.
- **Helps Gain Control.** It helps you gain control over necessary and un-necessary expenses while working toward debt elimination. Budgeting places you in the drivers' seat of your finances instead of your money dictating what you can and cannot do.
- **Organizes Finances.** Organizing your finances by creating a budget provides early warning signals for potential financial problems. Not only can a budget by design provide you with a record of all of your monetary transactions, it also acts as a guide for paying bills and immediately alerts you to the fact of potential problems occurring from overspending.

> A BUDGET GIVES YOU THE ABILITY TO MAKE INFORMED SPENDING DECISIONS AT ANY GIVEN TIME.

- **Offers Opportunities.** It gives you the ability to make informed spending decisions at any given time. Since you would know exactly where you stand when it comes to your finances, it offers the opportunity or chance to take advantage of prospects you may otherwise miss.

- **Provides Definite Objectives.** A budget assists you in striving toward financial goals. This process will help you stay focused and on task.
- **Provides More Money.** The greatest benefit of all for creating a budget is having extra money you never had before. Identifying and cutting back on unnecessary spending will save a ton of money over time. Paying your bills on time will not only save money, it will positively affect your credit and raise your credit score.

Your savings can be placed toward paying off a debt, or stashed away in some type of savings account building interest. Let your money work for you for a change.

87.
Build Financial Strength

*Make strong, intentional decisions that are based
on good habits that model responsible behavior.
Grow your financial strength. Build reserves.*

Have you developed good habits that model responsible behavior, and do you have a healthy attitude about money? Are you growing toward financial strength?

Being strong financially requires making sound intentional decisions. Make calculated risks that don't leave you too exposed. It includes building net worth as well as having good cash flow. Being strong financially will get you through the tough times that are bound to come when economies change, life changes, and circumstances happen that are often beyond your control.

> **BEING STRONG FINANCIALLY REQUIRES MAKING SOUND INTENTIONAL DECISIONS.**

When you aren't financially strong, you may be forced to make short-term decisions that aren't necessarily the right ones. If you are smart, have your money work for you, and keep your personal recourse debt ratio low, you'll take a tremendous amount of pressure off of yourself.

Being strong financially is something within your control. It will help weather storms and allow you to make better decisions for your future.

"Closing out Monthly Books," from Michael Cappuccio
- Measure gains and losses before it's too late.
- You can never make too much money, but you can always lose too much money.
- At the end of each month, close books, print income statements, and

balance sheets. This will allow you to measure gains and losses and evaluate what adjustments are needed moving forward.

"Monthly Financials with 'Rolling Twelve,'" from Richard Harshaw

- Financials should be prepared at least monthly; the P&L should have a new column called "Rolling Twelve," which shows the full fiscal year for consistency in analysis.
- Accurate job estimating; real-time "heads up" display of what is happening. Most in-office software packages have this option built into the reports menu.

88.

Be Financially Strong (Not Necessarily Super Rich)

*Being financially solid, having the right attitude
about money, and exercising good habits are deeply
important to your future, security, and mental freedom.*

How is your financial strength? Do you find that you and your family are growing in that area, or are you constantly facing financial pressure? Nothing can sabotage success any faster than succumbing to the negative energy and emotions that come with financial stress.

> FINANCIAL STRENGTH
> PRODUCES A MENTAL
> FREEDOM THAT ALLOWS
> YOU TO FOCUS ON THINGS
> THAT ARE IMPORTANT
> (AT A DIFFERENT LEVEL),
> LIKE RELATIONSHIPS AND
> HELPING OTHER PEOPLE.

I want to emphasize the importance of developing habits of good financial behavior that will produce financial strength. Financial strength produces a mental freedom that allows you to focus on things that are important (at a different level), like relationships and helping other people.

There are the obvious habits that model responsible financial behavior, such as creating a budget and using allowances for each category that work for you and your family; building up savings and reserves; purchasing in relation to your income and net worth; and being on top of your banking and credit activity. But there may be some other urgent matters you either have not thought of or have been putting off.

Think about any wills, trusts, or estate transfers you need to make to secure the future financial strength of your family. Tap into the advice of an attorney or financial advisor to find out the specific needs of your family, and then act on their advice! Procrastination in this area can lead to financial ruin and devastation for your family in the event of a catastrophic event!

Sometimes it's not bad financial habits as much as it is your attitude about money that stands in the way of your success. If you think money is the answer to all of your problems, then you're looking in the wrong direction for your source of happiness. Money is important and essential for living, but an unhealthy lust for more and more will bring the exact opposite of your desire for happiness.

Greed leads to a lifestyle of "more about me and less about others." The right attitude about money can actually assure our freedom from financial bondage.

Aren't your future and the security of your family worth making whatever changes you need to make to achieve financial strength?

89.
Constantly Be Building Your Business to Have More Value

Clearer thinking, better decisions, provision for unexpected or costly transition issues, continuity of business success—these are all benefits from "planning" to have more value.

At some point in your business career, it will likely be time to either retire or sell your business. You want to be continually building your business to have more value so that when that time comes, you can either transition to an heir in the best possible light or that you can get the most from your business in a sale.

Hire a business transition specialist to help you build a transition plan that addresses your financial needs, taxation issues for heirs, assurance of professional continuity, buy-sell insurance issues, leadership planning, and a host of other critical factors.

We are entering the second transition of the HVAC businesses as sons and daughters (who inherited the businesses from their fathers) plan on passing the concern on to their heirs or outside investors; a smooth transition helps assure the stability of the Mitsubishi Contractor base.

Here are some ways to increase the value of your business:

- Have a unique product.
- Differentiate yourself with your services.
- Develop a best-in-class team with highly trained employees.
- Establish a solid representation with references and referrals, and be known in the community.
- Exploit and utilize technology to your advantage.
- Build strong strategic partnerships with manufacturers, suppliers, and other vendors.

EXECUTE

90.
Have a "Get It Done Now" Mindset

Stop making excuses and get it done! Quite simply,
the difference between successful and unsuccessful people is
that successful people achieve predetermined results—they do
things now, they act, and they execute.

Always strive to satisfy the customer

Stop making excuses and get it done! Quite simply, the difference between successful and unsuccessful people is that successful people achieve predetermined results. You cannot execute, achieve, and make results happen without being really clear about what you want.

What if you were are charged with an important task? Are you capable and willing and do you have the ability to execute? Do you just think about doing it, or are you actually doing it?

It's the earliest version of Nike's philosophy: "Just Do It." Indeed, when we are acting on a request or striving to reach a personal objective, is there any other approach to even consider? Just do it. Get it done. Focus, power through, and succeed.

> **THE DIFFERENCE BETWEEN SUCCESSFUL AND UNSUCCESSFUL PEOPLE IS THAT SUCCESSFUL PEOPLE ACHIEVE PREDETERMINED RESULTS.**

Value a capacity for independent action, moral intelligence, a strength of will, and a willingness to cheerfully catch hold and lift.

When you're next faced with a task, project, assignment, big meeting, you name it—either for yourself or on behalf of another—take action. Start at the beginning and deploy High Leverage Activities (HLAs) to get the most out of your action, effort, and resources (see #35). If you feel stuck, commit to even fifteen minutes of action; you'll see that you often get caught up in the task and make tremendous progress. Your colleagues, owners, clients, shareholders, and board will value this attention to action and commitment to overcoming whatever obstacles, uncertainties, or questions surround the task in front of you.

Let your brand grow and more and more people will count on you to get things done, to succeed where they cannot, and to not clutter delegation by creating more issues, excuses, and mental roadblocks. Personally and professionally, become someone people can rely upon. This is creating a reputation of execution, and it is just as valuable now as it was two generations ago.

Go forward and create your powerful mindset, your reputation of execution. This will increase your personal success, since creating wins for others makes you indispensable.

91.
Execute with
Accountability

A great plan should include measurement and accountability with clarity on what, who, when, why, and how.

Clarity and focus are nothing without execution. Execution is doing. Executing with speed is to accelerate action. When you have clarity, you know what you want to achieve. You are able to put it in writing, and you are able to specifically communicate the "why" of it to those you need to work with to execute the vision. When you and your team have this ability, it is the result of having what I call "Strategic Clarity." How clear are you about what you really want? Our research and experience with hundreds of top performers indicates that most people have less clarity than they think they have. As a result they have difficulty pulling their teams together and frequently get the wrong results.

> YOU CAN CREATE THE GREATEST PLAN IN THE WORLD AND ESTABLISH THE MOST FOCUSED GOALS IMAGINABLE, BUT IF YOU FAIL TO EXECUTE THE PLAN YOU WILL NOT ACHIEVE IT.

The distinction for getting the right results faster is execution. You can create the greatest plan in the world and establish the most focused goals imaginable, but if you fail to execute the plan you will not achieve it. Every business has at least one strategic plan in its file cabinet that never became a reality.

What is the biggest reason plans fail to be executed? By far the biggest culprit is a communication disconnect between those who conceive the vision and those who must turn it into reality. You want execution to ensure clarity and leverage peer accountability. This happens by constantly sharing the action lens in front of your team, discussing what's done and what's not. Pretty simple and yet powerfully effective.

Invariably, when businesses conduct internal effectiveness surveys, poor communication is usually one of the top three problems identified.

To achieve the right results faster, leaders must continually cascade their vision down through the organization (small or large) so that every team member understands and supports it. This is not an easy thing to do and is the reason so many organizations struggle with it. Communication problems and challenges are found in every nook and cranny of our lives, from meetings to email, from text to voicemail. Each communication challenge impacts execution.

STRATEGIC CLARITY IS ACHIEVED WHEN YOU HAVE A CLEAR VIEW OF YOUR VISION AND UNDERSTAND WHAT YOU REALLY WANT, WHY YOU WANT IT, THE VALUE OF DOING IT, AND THE HIGHEST PURPOSE FOR DOING IT.

–TONY JEARY

Though clarity, focus, and execution are strongly linked and all three are important, the most significant is execution because execution is about doing. Clarity and focus provide a roadmap for the basis for doing what you need to do, but execution is about actually doing it; and this is where you will spend the bulk of your time.

Regardless of your role or vision, we all know we need others' assistance and cooperation to be highly successful; and your ability to persuade has a lot to do with others' willingness not only to assist you, but also to exceed expectations. When you can persuade others to exceed expectations, you take execution to a higher level and really move the results needle. The most successful people can effectively convince and persuade other people to take action on their behalf.

92.
Work the Plan, Utilize a Scorecard (Overall and for Each Team Member)

Having a scorecard allows all team members to visually see how their piece fits into the overall success of the plan and better manager their own efforts.

One of the biggest issues surrounding execution is the failure of accountability. Failure of accountability leads to people not taking action.

We recommend you take your plan and build it into a scorecard system where (as simple as it sounds), people's names are connected to specific actions. Whether they be tactics or strategies, there are actions that need to be deployed to be able to make the scorecard come to life and the results happen. Track goals, benchmarks, and individual progress.

Having a scorecard also allows all team members to visually see how their piece fits into the overall success of the plan. A great rule is for each plan to have a scorecard attached and an agreed-upon timeframe for completion. This allows for peer accountability, which supports proper execution.

A sample scorecard is available to download free in the Mitsubishi Contractor Toolkit at www.mitsubishipro.com/toolkit.

93.
Operate with a
Sense Of Urgency

Contractors must have a sense of urgency in responding to customer requests for information, pricing, and follow-up after the sale is closed. Speed of response creates a competitive advantage.

The pure definition of the word urgency is "of pressing importance." In today's world of technology where there is instant access to virtually everything at your fingertips, both life and business move faster than ever before, and this is a trend that will only continue. Speed, agility, and a proactive attitude are necessary requirements for survival and success. Urgency is continually acting as if things really matter—that they're important.

Operating with a sense of urgency does not mean having chaos or being frantic; it means that having a sincere drive to reach goals and serve your customers will lead to results. In a service business, operating with a sense of urgency will create a highly productive workplace; and, even more importantly, it will allow you to serve more customers, faster. When you have something broken in your home, what do you want? Speed. You want it fixed now.

> **OPERATING WITH A SENSE OR URGENCY— IMPORTANCE—IS A CONTAGIOUS LEADERSHIP TRAIT.**

In the book *The Road Ahead,* Bill Gates said that a secret to Microsoft's success is they always think of themselves as being on the losing side, and this makes them strive to be number one every day. This attitude creates a sense of urgency, which makes them work hard to survive in the highly competitive environment of the IT industry.

HEALTH

94.
Live Healthy!

Truly successful people live healthy, eat well, exercise, manage stress, rest, relax, de-stress, and breathe well, so they can think, act, and thrive at peak performance.

Healthy people understand their body and the triggers that lead to stress. They avoid those triggers, and work to incorporate a positive mental attitude and healthy positive habits into their life.

Do you understand your body? Do you know what foods make you feel tired, bloated, and fatigued and what foods lead to a healthy, energetic day? Do you know what foods have a high glycemic index and cause you to store fat?

So many people don't. But when you begin to understand how your body works, reacts, and feels, you'll make better food choices. You'll know what foods are best for you and which ones to avoid. You'll know when you feel more energy, and you'll exercise

> YOU WANT TO BE FINANCIALLY HEALTHY, SURE. BUT YOU ALSO WANT TO BE PHYSICALLY, EMOTIONALLY, AND SPIRITUALLY HEALTHY.

at that time of day. You'll know when you think better, and more clearly, and you'll schedule work during those times. Understanding your mind and body is key; and then, guess what—as a leader, your people will often follow you.

Successful people are attracted to healthy people. Why? Because people want more of what you have; if you're unhealthy they don't want it. It's pretty simple. After years of coaching high achievers to earn more, learn more, and get more results, one of the interesting commonalities

I (Tony) observed is the need for a healthier life. Many entrepreneurs or CEOs neglect their mental and physical health when they're striving for financial success. Does that sound like you?

We have both been focused on health for a decade or more. Eventually after reaching financial success you get to a point where you become more focused on holistic success. You want to be financially healthy, sure. But you also want to be physically, emotionally, and spiritually healthy.

> A HEALTHY BODY IS THE START TO A HEALTHY MIND AND A HEALTHY SOUL.
>
> –PETER THOMAS

We have both written books about wellness. In my (Peter's) *LifePilot* program, I teach entrepreneurs how to advance and excel creating clarity of values, and then use my own example of health. And I (Tony) wrote a book called *Ultimate Health* to help me mentor and coach others to success in the area of physical wellness.

Living healthy also means aligning your values to your daily activities. Get complete clarity on what you want and then live your life that way. In order to live a healthier life in all quadrants, you have to pay attention to those things that matter.

95.
Manage Stress

One of the major causes of disease, aging, and death is stress. Be smart, live smart, and lead and model healthy thinking.

One of the major causes of disease, aging, and death is stress. Stress occurs when our mental, physical, or spiritual challenges exceed our ability to cope with them. Stress kills—literally. And it kills morale, too. On the personal side, it causes your body to secrete hormones that can have a negative impact on your health. On the organizational side, stress can cause turnover and burnout, and it can even weaken execution.

When you can reduce stress, everything flows much more smoothly. Your business life, your relationships, and your physical well-being will all improve. Stress can be situational and caused by several factors, including how we plan, react, and cope with what we allow in our lives.

There will always be obstacles and issues in life that are outside your control. But those are externally driven, isolated events. Stress is what happens when pressure builds in the gap between the things we want to do and the things we are actually doing. It results from a lack of congruence between the life you want, your goals, and the life you live.

> **STRESS IS WHAT HAPPENS WHEN PRESSURE BUILDS IN THE GAP BETWEEN THE THINGS WE WANT TO DO AND THE THINGS WE ARE ACTUALLY DOING.**

The best way to cure stress is to drill down to the source of the problem, and cut stress out before it even happens. If you do an "audit" and make a list of the top ten most stressful things that happen on a daily basis, you will begin to discover a lot of opportunities to make a difference. By changing certain habits, you can often eliminate most sources of stress in your life.

Your true wealth is determined by the amount of things you do not have to worry about. Worry is a stressor. Often, the most frequent stressor in anyone's life is a lack of time. But a lack of time is not actually producing the stress; it is the way you are managing your time. In that moment of rushing, you are stressed because you have a lack of time. But in the moments leading up to it, you had plenty. Building "margin time" into your life right now is one of the fastest ways to eliminate stress. Another reason to build margin time is to make room for life's unexpected events. Without a built-in margin time, people feel pressed and stressed. You owe it to yourself to live as stress free as possible.

> ELIMINATE STRESS; YOUR TRUE WEALTH IS DETERMINED BY THE AMOUNT OF THINGS YOU DO NOT HAVE TO WORRY ABOUT.
> –TONY JEARY

Stress is a big factor in many health issues. Some stress is unavoidable; by learning to manage it well we can minimize the negative effects on our bodies and still maintain a healthy and happy lifestyle. Eating right, exercising, and getting enough sleep are great ways to control stress, as well as relaxing with deep-breathing exercises, massage therapy, or stretching. (Stretching increases your energy, improves your flexibility, helps your coordination, and reduces muscle tension. It's a great stress reliever! Remember my daily performance standards? One of them is to stretch, flex, and breathe with confidence. I make it a practice to do these things daily.) Or you may need to do something externally, like getting a healthy hobby or an outlet by helping others.

You can also learn to eliminate stress from your personal and professional relationships. I made a comment once that you can always be right or you can have a great marriage; the same truth applies in all of your relationships. It's often just not worth the stress to argue. Sometimes you may just need to learn to compromise.

When I was about thirty-five years old I was playing golf at a prestigious golf course in town; and instead of enjoying the beautiful day, I was focused on having to fire someone at my office. It was really gnawing on me until my friend gave me some great advice: When you're forced to make tough decisions like that, make them and move on. Don't allow them to pull you down and keep you down. I've used that great advice many times in my life since then.

One of the best ways to prosper, grow, and win is to determine that you will not worry about the tough decisions and negative situations or let them control your emotions, your thoughts, and your energy.

96.
Keep Health and Energy Management Top of Mind

Managing health and energy will help you operate at peak performance and maximize top opportunities.

A leader's health routine matters! In fact, health and energy management has become one of the top five most solicited areas.

There are so many parts to this puzzle: stress management; diet; exercise (cardio, resistance, balance, and stretching); removing toxins from your life; visualization; sleep; and, heck, even saying "no" to many things. But your life, health, and happiness should be a priority.

Success starts with awareness, followed by knowledge, then a healthful and energetic lifestyle. Healthy people drive results! We are all creatures of habit and many fail in this area. They do not think about the consequences of those habits. You need to expand your awareness of what you need to do to improve your health; then develop the right habits.

97.
Focus on Feeding Your Mind to Avoid Stagnation

Feeding your mind ensures you are constantly incorporating innovation, growth, and new learning into your life.

Powerful leaders who get real results avoid stagnation by seeking constant fresh inputs and self-improvement. New information can be gathered through reading trade and industry magazines, newspapers, books, and other publications—including brief recaps or abstracts that save time by condensing information.

Coaches and mentors are also a great way to learn and grow. By listening to and observing the habits of those more successful than yourself in selected areas, and then modeling that behavior, you will constantly elevate your levels of thought, skill, process, and tools.

Developing a team around you that is constantly feeding you new information will ensure you are continually poised to make effective, smart decisions. Whether this is insight into your own organization, the competition, or areas of interest/research, keeping abreast of those important data points is a key distinction and descriptor of an effective leader—and a sharp mind.

98.
Conduct a
Health Assessment

*Having a strong mind and body directly affects
your ability to execute your goals effectively.*

Most people get busy with their life and oftentimes leave health as "less than top priority." We believe health is a big piece to the successful life puzzle of getting what you want. Having a strong mind and body directly affects your ability to execute your goals.

Below are specific areas of opportunity in the area of ultimate health. List what you are doing now and what you want to do in each area.

#	Health Area	Rating (1-5)	What You Are Doing Now	What You Want to Do
1.	Lifestyle			
2.	Mental Management			
3.	Ultimate Longevity			
4.	Stress Management			
5.	Immune System			
6.	Testing			
7.	Exercise			
8.	Oral			
9.	Eyes/ Vision			
10.	Toxin Management			
11.	Hormone Management			
12.	Vitamins			
13.	Caloric Management			
14.	Ear, Nose, and Throat			
15.	Food			
16.	Skin			
17.	Fluids			
18.	Emotions			
19.	Sleep			
20.	Spiritual Wellness			

Visit www.ultimatehealth-book.com

99.
Know Your Personal Energy Cycle

Use your peak energy times to focus on High Leverage Activities (HLAs) to maximize your effectiveness.

When determining your priorities and scheduling your time, take into consideration your personal energy cycle. Some people perform better early in the morning; some perform better mid-day or late at night. Recent studies have even suggested that Tuesday is the most productive day of the week for many people.

You maximize your time if you identify your personal energy cycle and schedule activities appropriately. Use this chart as your guide.

Energy Levels

HIGH	AVERAGE
✓ New Learning ✓ Complex Activities	✓ Everyday Activities ✓ Non-Complex Assignments
BELOW AVERAGE	LOW
✓ Routine Tasks ✓ Meetings	✓ Easy Activities ✓ Routine Tasks ✓ Tasks requiring little thought

On a scale of 1 to 10, with 1 being "poor" and 10 being "excellent," rate yourself in each of the following areas. After you have rated yourself in each area, review those areas with a score of 8 or below. In the space provided, estimate the amount of time you could save each day if you were to improve your skills in the area.

#	Questions	Rating Est.	Time Gained
1.	I begin and/or end each day by developing a to-do list.	1 2 3 4 5 6 7 8 9 10	
2.	I review my to-do list and prioritize by those issues most important *and* urgent.	1 2 3 4 5 6 7 8 9 10	
3.	I set specific times each day for routine tasks like returning phone calls and dealing with email.	1 2 3 4 5 6 7 8 9 10	
4.	I understand my personal energy cycle and schedule important and urgent tasks during times when my energy level is highest.	1 2 3 4 5 6 7 8 9 10	
5.	I prioritize my reading/research and have learned to skim those articles that can be and fully read only what will be give me real value.	1 2 3 4 5 6 7 8 9 10	
6.	I ask people to send me only relevant information/mail/email.	1 2 3 4 5 6 7 8 9 10	
7.	I use a "time planning" system such as a Day Timer or calendar to help prioritize daily events.	1 2 3 4 5 6 7 8 9 10	
8.	I prioritize and gain time by screening visitors/calls and only take those that move me towards accomplishing my goals.	1 2 3 4 5 6 7 8 9 10	
9.	I have well developed, written short and long-term goals with actions for accomplishing each.	1 2 3 4 5 6 7 8 9 10	
10.	I am able to purge my to-do list of tasks that are less important and not urgent and will not have an impact on my overall success if they are not done.	1 2 3 4 5 6 7 8 9 10	

100.
Maximize Your Metabolism and Eliminate Toxins

Spend some time thinking about changes you need to make to be able to leverage a healthy lifestyle, and continue to add good habits while removing bad ones.

Your metabolism is what converts your body's food into fuel, or energy. The best way to make your metabolism work for you is to be aware of your eating habits and balance them with healthy, efficient exercise. You can achieve your health and fitness goals without starving yourself on a strict diet and then suffering the consequences of it later.

Maximize your metabolism by making a few simple changes:

- Start an aerobics or a cardio exercise routine so you burn more calories right away.
- Start strength training (or weight training) to build muscles that will boost your metabolism in the long run.
- Form healthy eating habits that are both realistic and permanent.

Find an exercise or training regimen that works for you, your body, your goals, and your schedule. Then stick to it! Don't try to re-create the wheel; there are many great programs out there that do not cost all that much, or that you can find for free on the Internet. Whatever you choose, make sure it is high quality and that thousands of others have experienced success with it too.

If you want to achieve excellent health in every area of your life, you must become aware of and eliminate toxins—and that can be stress, chemicals, people, habits, attitudes, or anything else that drags you down and keeps you from being the best you can be. As far as chemical toxins, it goes without saying that they can ruin your health and your life and must be eliminated at all costs. When I decided to take my health seriously, I started eating organic food and wild-caught fish, versus farm-raised; and I very seldom have a soda or junk food.

Toxic people are another subject; sometimes people can actually be toxic to your success. When I make a phone call and I find that the person I'm speaking with has a wrong attitude (often I can detect it in their tone of voice), rather than argue or complain I'll usually just politely hang up and call back to speak to someone else.

I like to be around people who smile a lot (if I'm talking to them over the phone, I can tell if they're smiling with their voices), because they bring positive energy and not a toxic, negative attitude. I like hanging out with people who have good habits—who show up on time, who are cheerful, and who follow through with their promises—because I only want good habits to rub off on me (and my family).

Today spend some time thinking about any changes you need to make to be able to leverage a healthy lifestyle. Are you eating the right foods and exercising regularly? Are you managing stress well? Are you getting enough rest?

If there are any toxins—either chemical or individual—focus on eliminating them from your life. Albert Einstein once said, "Weakness of *attitude* becomes weakness of character." It's up to you to monitor your own attitude and the attitude of the people around you.

Conclusion

We hope you have found this work valuable. In fact, we hope you keep this book and refer to it often. You may even consider starting a 30-day challenge—as you read through the contents, pick 30 of the 100 lessons and tips that resonate with you most, and study one for each day for the next 30 days.

We also encourage you to go online and download the free MEHVAC Contractor Kit. This great tool has 17 of the items we discussed in this book in e-format so you can use them immediately.

Stay connected to Mitsubishi Electric and make ductless an even bigger part of your future. It's where U.S. air conditioning is going and we don't want you to be left behind. We want you to be ahead! (To look into the benefits of being a Mitsubishi Diamond Contractor, download the Diamond Contractor brochure from the Mitsubishi Contractor Toolkit at www.mistubishipro.com/toolkit.)

Stay in touch, too. Peter and I enjoy impacting entrepreneurs and leaders, and we welcome emails sharing successes you have and ways we might be of service to you. Contact me at Info@tonyjeary.com.

We appreciate teaming with MEHVAC and their enthusiastic support in making this vision a reality. Their commitment to encourage and educate contractors as they continue to grow is unsurpassed.

Use these lessons and watch your business grow. May this year be your best year ever.

Appendix:

Tony's best year ever: https://www.youtube.com/playlist?list=PL3Ht MqjJd94xjnAkNDsR6RIOE1ClqkY_H

Ensure strategic alignment between your branding, marketing, and sales.

Marketing Audit:

#	Collateral Item (What)	Rating 1-10	Purpose (Notes)	Action (How)	Budget
		Marketing Collateral Audit			
		1. CLARITY			
1.	Branding Matrix (see kit)				
2.	Strategic Business Plan				
3.	Logo				
4.	Value Proposition or Unique Selling Position (USP)				
5.	Slogan/Jingle/Tagline*				
6.	Color Scheme*				
7.	Competitive Comparison				
		2. BASE COMMUNICATION			
8.	Stationery: Letterhead, Envelopes & Mailing Labels*				
9.	Fax Cover Sheet				
10.	Business Cards				
11.	Christmas Cards				
12.	Brochure(s)*				
13.	One sheets*				
14.	Press Kit				
15.	Newsletter				
16.	Business Reply Card				
17.	Direct Mail Pieces				
18.	Stationery: Thank You Cards				
19.	Pitch Book				
20.	Brag Book				
21.	Exterior Signs				
22.	Vehicle Identification				
23.	Interior Signs				
		3. ELECTRONIC/WEB			
24.	Website				
25.	Auto Responders				
26.	Social Media				
27.	Blogs				
28.	YouTube				
29.	YouTube Channel				
30.	E-mail Stationary (electronic letterhead)				
31.	Power Point Message				
32.	Video				
33.	Telephone System Messages -- On Hold and Voice Mail				

	4. VEHICLE				
34.	Vehicle Wraps				
35.	Bumper Stickers				
36.	Magnetic Signs				
37.	Window Decal				
	5. RESOURCES & ARCHIVES				
38.	Photo Library				
39.	References/Testimonial Letters				
40.	Database				
41.	Database Software				
42.	Case Studies				
	6. MERCHANDISING / GIVE-AWAYS				
43.	Trade Show Materials				
44.	Pop-Ups				
45.	Calculator				
46.	T-Shirts				
47.	Hats				
48.	Banners and signs				
49.	Bumper Stickers				
50.	Calendars				
51.	Door Hangers				
52.	Newspaper Inserts				
	7. PRESS AND COMMUNITY RELATIONS				
53.	Articles and Columns Written				
54.	Reprints				
55.	Organizations and Affiliations				
56.	Community Involvement				
57.	Feature Stories				
58.	Awards Received				
	8. PUBLISHING				
59.	Handbook				
60.	White Paper				
	9. EVENTS & TRAINING				
61.	Tent Cards				
62.	Follow – Up				
63.	Lunch & Learn Kits				
	10. INSTITUTIONAL ADVERTISING				
64.	Classified Ads				
65.	Yellow Pages				
	11. INTERNAL MARKETING				
66.	Signs in Vehicles				
67.	Scorecard				
68.	Storyboard				

Business Ground Rules Toolkit

1. MOLO your life and business (More of, Less of) - TEMPLATE

2. Pre-make installation kits for selected jobs so they are ready to go prior to install – SAMPLE LISTS

3. Prefered customer agreements – SAMPLE

4. Ensure strategic alignment between your branding, marketing and sales – VISUAL

5. Survey your company culture – SAMPLE

6. Work the plan, utilize a scorecard (overall and for each team member) - TEMPLATE and EXAMPLES

7. Branding Matrix – TOOL FOR DEVELOPING YOUR BRAND

8. Marketing Audit – ELECTRONIC VERSION OF PREVIOUS AUDIT SHOWN

9. MORE TO COME HERE

Organizations, Associations & Training

Tony Jeary
Tony Jeary International
Info@tonyjeary.com
www.tonyjeary.com
817.430.9422
TJI is a boutique agency surrounding Tony Jeary - The RESULTS Guy™. We change or expand top performers' thinking as well as their organizations so they accomplish their visions faster. For three decades Tony has positively impacted both small and large organizations, both new and mature and both domestic and international. Our core methodology is *Strategic Acceleration* - Results Faster through Clarity - Focus – Execution.

Mitsubishi Trainings
There are multiple contractor training opportunities with Mitsubishi Electric. Visit www.mitsubishipro.com/en/professional/professional-training/overview-for details, time and options.

Become a Diamond Contractor: The Diamond Contractor program is a network of hundreds of independent Residential HVAC Contractors located around the country. These Contractors have received special training to install and service the Mitsubishi M&P product line. They are committed to making Mitsubishi Cooling and Heating a major portion of their business. Diamond Contractors have access to special marketing tools, specialized training, and additional sales and application support.

Weldon Long (contributor to the book)
Weldon@weldonlong.com
The Weldon Long Organization
1115 Elkton Drive #402
Colorado Springs, CO 80907
www.weldonlong.com
Office: (719) 304-5300
Fax: (719) 465-5801

The HVAC Sales Academy was created by Weldon Long to give HVAC contractors ONLINE access to powerful HVAC Sales and Service Technician training programs without expensive travel or extended time out of the field. Ongoing weekly coaching programs ensure the sales and service technician revenue enhancing programs are actually implemented at the kitchen table with homeowners - where it matters most. Weldon Long is one of the nation's leading experts in selling residential HVAC systems. His new book, *The Power of Consistency*, is a *NY Times* and *Wall Street Journal* national bestseller.

Richard Harshaw (contributor to the book)
Lodestar Consulting Systems
4625 East Brilliant Sky Drive
Cave Creek, Arizona 85331
www.lodestarconsultinginc.com/richard_harshaw
480-227-7231

Lodestar specializes in sales rep development for distributors, and also conducts contractor-oriented training.

Mike Cappuccio (contributor to the book)
www.netrinc.com
mikecap@pacbell.net
Phone: (781) 933-6387
Fax: (781) 933-4727
165A New Boston Street, Woburn, MA 01801

Michael Cappuccio is one of New England's largest and most successful air conditioning and refrigeration dealers. Cappuccio is President of N.E.T.R. Inc. Air Conditioning & Refrigeration in Woburn, Mass.; and, as a Mitsubishi Diamond Dealer, he enjoys consulting, advising, and sharing best practices with contractors all around the US.

Nexstar Network
www.nexstarnetwork.com
888.609.5490
Nexstar Network has been trusted by contractors to help them grow their business since 1992. Founded and owned by members, Nextstar Network partners with nearly 500 top independent home services contractors in plumbing, heating, air conditioning, and electrical trades.

Quality Service Contractors "QSC"
180 South Washington Street
Suite 100
Falls Church, VA 22046
www.qsc-phcc.org
Phone 1: (800)533-7694
Phone 2: (703)237-8100
Fax: (703)237-7442
E-mail: quality@qsc-phcc.org
Charlie Wallace, VP/COO
QSC functions as a self-supporting business unit of the Plumbing-Heating-Cooling-Contractors National Association. All funds generated from its membership remain with the organization; they are used only for initiatives selected and approved by the membership. QSC enhances both the industry, and its members' reputations by originating and delivering timely and lively professional and educational training programs. In most cases, this instruction is available nowhere else.

ABOUT THE AUTHORS

Tony Jeary

Tony Jeary is a strategist. Many call him The RESULTS Guy™ because of this simple fact—he helps clients get the right results faster. He is a unique and powerful facilitator and subject matter expert who has advised over 1,000 clients and published over 3 dozen books. His studio process of live note taking, combined with his *Strategic Acceleration* methodology, is a secret weapon for his special clients. Tony has invested the past 20 years developing facilitation processes and systems that allow him and his team to accelerate results, doing planning meetings in a single day, and producing results in a single eight-hour session that often otherwise take days, weeks, and months. That's a rare gift.

The world's greatest leaders recognize the importance of thinking, strategy, and communication; and many seek Tony for all three of these. He's a gifted encourager who helps clarify visions.

The primary goal of all leader is to enhance value and communicate their vision effectively so that their teams can execute that vision in the marketplace. He does this, personally coaching presidents and CEOs of Walmart, TGI Friday's, New York Life, Firestone, Samsung, Ford, Texaco, and SAM's; even those on the Forbes richest 400 engage Tony for his advice. Tony personally helps these top leaders: define their goals; accelerate their opportunities; create, establish, and build their personal brands and careers; deliver powerful paradigm-shifting presentations; grow their leadership abilities; and accelerate the right results faster! He and/or his whole firm can be booked through his business manager. Tony Jeary International can be retained to do amazing things to support accelerated RESULTS. Learn more at www.tonyjeary.com.

Peter Thomas

Peter Thomas has been a serial entrepreneur for more than four decades, specializing in franchising and real estate. Peter is recognized as one of the leading developers and lenders of his time in North America. He has developed billions of dollars in real estate projects, from shopping centers, apartments, and condominiums, to golf courses.

Peter is the past Chairman and Founder of Century 21 Real Estate Canada Ltd., founded Samoth Capital Corporation, a Canadian public real estate company now known as Sterling Centrecorp Inc., and developed the Four Seasons Resort in Scottsdale, Arizona.

For his philanthropic contributions to society, Peter was recognized with the prestigious 2010 National Caring Award, an honor shared by Lance Armstrong, General Colin Powell, and Laura Bush.

Peter is the Chairman Emeritus of the Entrepreneurs' Organization and the bestselling author of two Canadian books, *Never Fight with a Pig* and *Be Great*. For further information please visit www.lifepilot.org.

Currently, Peter serves as Chairman and CEO of Thomas Franchise Solutions Ltd. and as a Director for the TFS Fund. Peter was very proud to be awarded his Honorary Doctorate of Laws LLD from the Royal Roads University in Victoria, British Columbia, for his work with the creation of *LifePilot* (www.lifepilot.org) and for his other charity works.

Notes

Notes